large-as-life
BIBLE ADVENTURES

13 AMAZING "YOU-ARE-THERE" BIBLE EXPERIENCES

Loveland, Colorado

www.group.com

Group resources actually work!

This Group resource helps you focus on **"The 1 Thing®"**—a life-changing relationship with Jesus Christ. "The 1 Thing" incorporates our **R.E.A.L.** approach to ministry. It reinforces a growing friendship with Jesus, encourages long-term learning, and results in life transformation, because it's:

Relational
Learner-to-learner interaction enhances learning and builds Christian friendships.

Experiential
What learners experience through discussion and action sticks with them up to 9 times longer than what they simply hear or read.

Applicable
The aim of Christian education is to equip learners to be both hearers and doers of God's Word.

Learner-based
Learners understand and retain more when the learning process takes into consideration how they learn best.

Large-As-Life Bible Adventures
Copyright © 2007 Group Publishing, Inc.

All rights reserved. No part of this book may be reproduced in any manner whatsoever without prior written permission from the publisher, except where noted in the text and in the case of brief quotations embodied in critical articles and reviews. For information, e-mail Permissions at inforights@group.com or write Permissions, Group Publishing, Inc., Product Support Services Dept., P.O. Box 481, Loveland, CO 80539.

Visit our Web site: www.group.com

Credits
Chief Creative Officer: Joani Schultz
Contributing Authors: Jim Hawley, Mikal Keefer, Lois Keffer, and Jan Kershner
Children's Senior Developer: Patty Anderson
Children's Ministry Champion: Christine Yount Jones
Copy Editor: Dena Twinem
Art Director: Andrea Filer
Print Production Artist: Boven Design Studio, Inc.
Cover Designer: The DesignWorks Group
Illustrators: Bryan Bandyk, Amy Bryant, Dana Regan, and Drew Rose
Photographers: Rodney Stewart and Daniel Treat
Production Manager: DeAnne Lear

Unless otherwise indicated, all Scripture quotations are taken from the *Holy Bible*, New Living Translation, copyright © 1996, 2004. Used by permission of Tyndale House Publishers, Inc., Wheaton, Illinois 60189. All rights reserved.

ISBN 0-7644-3549-2
10 9 8 7 6 5 4 3 2 1   07 06 05
Printed in the United States of America.

Executive Producer: Thom Schultz
Producer: Brenda Kraft
Audio Producers: Brenda Kraft, John J. DiModica, Jeff Koska, Matt Schultz
Music Producer Tracks 19, 20: Jay Stocker for JaysPlace

NOTE: Track 10 - © 2004 by Group Publishing, Inc. All rights reserved. No authorized duplication permitted.

Contents

Introduction   5

OLD TESTAMENT

1 God saves Noah and the animals
Genesis 6:9–7:18   9

2 Baby Moses is saved from death
Exodus 1:1–2:10   13

3 God protects the Israelites from the plagues
Exodus 7:1–10:29   19

4 God spares the Israelites during Passover
Exodus 11:1–15:21   30

5 Gideon defeats the Midianites
Judges 7:1-22   36

6 Elijah confronts the prophets of Baal
1 Kings 18:1-40   42

7 Jonah disobeys God
Jonah 1–3   48

NEW TESTAMENT

8 Jesus calms a storm
Matthew 8:23-27   54

9 Peter walks to Jesus on the Sea of Galilee
Matthew 14:22-33   59

10 Men bring their friend to Jesus for healing
Luke 5:17-25   63

11 Jesus washes the disciples' feet
John 13:1-17   68

12 Jesus dies on the cross and rises again
Luke 23–24   71

13 Jesus appears to his followers as they fish
Matthew 28:18-20; John 21:1-17   76

Introduction

Congratulations! You now have at your fingertips 13 large-as-life, you-are-there Bible adventures. Use them to immerse, engulf, and surround your kids in Bible-times fun and learning. These high-impact, low-prep Bible adventures are just right for Sunday morning, Wednesday evening, summer fun—in fact, they're just right for any time!

These skits require minimal costumes, staff, or props. With a little bit of effort, you can turn a ho-hum Bible lesson into an unforgettable Bible adventure!

Here's how.

Keep the first thing first

What exactly is the "first thing"?

Hint: It's *not* the quality of your performance. You and your kids are under no pressure to put on a flawless production.

So relax…and focus instead on getting every child involved in each adventure. Because while the quality of the production isn't critical, the quality of the *learning* is, and involved children learn more and retain what they learn longer.

Use the debriefing questions provided at the end of each skit, and you'll engage children even more completely. You'll cement the learning even firmer in kids' minds and hearts.

Bring enthusiasm to your role

Your role as Narrator is an important role. The Narrator has the most difficult lines, directs the action, sets the pace, and acts as a prompter. If you're acting as the Narrator, you'll be able to manage the flow of the skit. And if you seem excited about the Bible adventure, kids will, too!

Another way to build excitement is to begin the adventure before the adventure. How can you do that? It's easy! Greet children outside your room to set the stage and build anticipation. Kids will be itching to get inside and start the fun!

Make it safe for children

Some children take to the stage like ducks to water. They *love* having the spotlight turned their direction. They're natural-born thespians.

But other children become anxious when asked to speak in front of a crowd…and in their minds, "crowd" means two or more people. For shy children, the notion of being in a skit inspires terror. So don't pressure children into roles. But do involve everyone in the adventure. And that's easy, because that's how these adventures have been constructed.

And each time you see the Allergy Alert symbol ⊕ in the margin, take the necessary precautions.

Be aware that some children have food allergies that can be dangerous. Know your children, and consult with parents about allergies their children may have. Also be sure to read food labels carefully as hidden ingredients can cause allergy-related problems.

Don't sweat the stage

In a perfect world, you have a large elevated area at one end of your room. It's lit professionally, and the sound technician takes care of all the microphones. Don't live in that world? Neither do most people.

All you need is an open area so kids can move around easily. We've provided all the details you need—complete with illustrations—to easily and quickly create amazing sets that kids will love. And they don't take forever to build or a lot of money to fund. We mean it when we say *easy*.

Use the CD to make adventures come alive

Most adventures come with sound effects or dramas that help set the stage and tell the story. Sometimes it's a background sound you'll play throughout the adventure. Other times it's a very specific drama sequence or sound effect you'll use to highlight an element of the narrative.

Place your CD player where you can easily reach it, and adjust the sound before the skit begins. The adventures will indicate when you need a helper to operate the CD player.

Finally—have fun!

Kids take their cues—literally and emotionally—from you. If you're having fun, your kids will, too.

So have an adventure with these Bible adventures…and enjoy leading your kids into a deeper understanding of these large-as-life Bible events!

A Word About Copying Scripts and CDs

Feel free to make as many photocopies of scripts as you desire for use in your own church's ministries. You have complete permission to do so, whether you need two scripts or 200.

The CD *can't* be legally reproduced, however. Use it in your ministry, but please don't burn additional copies.

Thanks for demonstrating integrity to the children you serve in how you use this ministry resource.

Bible Adventure 1

God saves Noah and the animals

Bible Basis: Genesis 6:9–7:18

Supplies

- Bible
- white inflated balloons
- filled squirt guns
- masking tape
- *Skits & Drama* CD: "Storm Sounds" (track 1)
- CD player

Preparation

Before class, clear furniture and other obstacles from the center of your room. Then use masking tape to make a large ark (or boat) shape in the middle of the floor.

Bible Adventure

Meet kids outside your room. When everyone has arrived,

say: **Today we're in for some stormy seas! We'd better hurry and get inside our boat. Actually, in this Bible story the boat is called an ark. No matter what it's called, it's the place to be with this big storm brewing. Let's hurry!**

Start to open the door, and then hesitate. **Oh, wait. I forgot to mention that you're all going to be** *animals* **in this Bible story. So get down on all fours so we can get going.**

Have kids crawl into the room, and direct them to quickly get inside the masking tape shape on the floor.

Open your Bible to Genesis 6 and show kids the chapter.

say: **This is the story of Noah and the ark. It's true because it comes straight from the Bible. I'm going to be the narrator for this story. That means I'll tell the story. But I'll need your help! You'll be the characters in the story. That means you have speaking parts. But don't worry, it's pretty simple stuff. Remember, I said you're animals!**

Here's what I need. I'll assign you a character according to the month in which you were born. Then, whenever the name of your animal is mentioned, you'll stand and sound off with that animal's noise. Ready?

Assign roles according to the following guidelines. Let kids practice their animal sounds a few times.

- January—dog
- February—cat
- March—owl
- April—lion
- May—pig
- June—cow
- July—chimpanzee
- August—sheep
- September—coyote
- October—horse
- November—fruit fly
- December—kangaroo (hop around)

say: **In the story, when we talk about thunder, make thunder by stomping your feet.** Have kids practice. **When we talk about clouds, I'll need your help in carefully moving the clouds across the sky.** Have kids practice waving their arms in the air. **One more thing about the sounds you're helping with: When I go like this** (cut-throat motion), **you'll need to stop the noise so the story can continue. Well, I think we're ready to start the story.**

Many years ago, the earth was bad. Only a man named Noah was good. God told Noah that he would bring a flood of waters upon the earth to destroy everything. God told Noah to build an ark so that Noah, his family, and two of every living creature would survive.

Noah obeyed. He built the ark and loaded the animals onto the ark two by two. First came the dogs (pause after each animal to hear all noises), **then the cats, then the owls, then the lions, then the pigs, then the cows, then the chimpanzees, then the sheep, then the coyotes, then the horses, then the fruit flies, and finally the kangaroos. When all the animals were loaded, they made a noise that could be heard for miles** (all animals sound off). **Soon darkness covered the sky** (turn off most of the lights).

Begin playing the "Storm Sounds" segment (track 1) from the CD. **Then huge clouds began coming in from the north.** (Push weather balloons gently over crowd.) **They rolled slowly across the sky. First one, then another. Soon the skies were filled with clouds. Never before had anyone seen clouds like these.**

Soon it began to lightning (turn lights on and off rapidly) **and thunder** (stomp feet).

The animals became frightened and began to cry out (all animals sound off).

Then came the rains (shoot squirt guns into air). **It rained for 40 days and 40 nights. The rains continued and filled all the streams and rivers and lakes and oceans. Finally the entire earth was covered with water.** Turn off the CD player.

After 40 days, the rains stopped (stop squirt guns). **And the clouds began moving back to where they came from** (have kids wave their arms to push balloons back). **Gradually the skies began to clear. The big rain clouds separated and disappeared, allowing the sun to shine** (turn on lights). **And the waters that covered the earth began to recede.**

When it was safe, Noah opened the door of the ark and began releasing the animals. First came the chimpanzees (pause after each animal), **then the cats, and the dogs, then horses, cows, and the lions, then the owls, and the sheep, then the coyotes, the pigs, and then two, no, three, no, five, no, a dozen, no, countless fruit flies, and of course the kangaroos. All of the animals were overjoyed to get out of the ark.**

God sent a sign in the sky—the rainbow—to show that he would never again destroy the earth with a flood. God blessed Noah's family. Noah and his family and the animals all went forth to live a happy life as they replenished the earth.

Have kids form pairs to discuss the following questions. After each question, invite partners to share their answers with the rest of the class.

ASK: • **If you had been Noah, what would you have said and done when God told you to build the ark?**

• **What do you think Noah's friends and neighbors thought when he began building the ark?**

• What word would you use to describe what the ark might have been like on the 39th day of rain?

• What is it like to see a rainbow and realize that it's a sign from God?

say: **God could have just destroyed the whole earth and everything in it, but he gave people a second chance. That's typical of God—he loves us and wants us to be his people. Let's pray for that right now.**

Close in prayer, thanking God for his rainbow promise and thanking him for loving us so much that he saved the earth and then sent his Son, Jesus, to save us from sin. Pray that each child in your class would come to know Jesus.

Bible Adventure 2

Baby Moses is saved from death

Bible Basis: Exodus 1:1–2:10

Supplies

- Bible
- empty produce boxes (with molded liners, if possible)
- couch or long table
- green construction paper
- bath-tissue tubes
- blue construction paper (if molded liners are not available)
- clear packing tape
- scissors
- utility knife
- artificial reeds and plants
- basket
- tunic, sash, sword, and sandals (for Egyptian Guard's costume)
- tunic, sash, jewelry, and sandals (for Pharaoh's Daughter's costume)
- construction paper
- pens
- two photocopies of "Finding Baby Moses" script (page 18)
- *Skits & Drama* CD: "Nile River" (track 2)
- CD player

Preparation

Begin collecting empty produce boxes from a grocery store a week or so before this lesson. Determine how many boxes you'll need to make a river that fits across one wall of the room. Some produce boxes, such as apple boxes, come with blue molded liners—ready-made "water" for your river! You'll also need several empty

13

bath tissue tubes.

Before this session, clear chairs and tables from the room. Then put together the "Nile" along one side of the room, about a foot or two away from the wall. Here's how to make the river: Gather enough produce boxes so that you can put them end to end along the length of one wall. Use the utility knife to cut down all four corners of the middle boxes so the box ends can be folded inside. On the end boxes, only cut the corners on one end. Tape the box ends down, then tape all the boxes together in a row to form a sort of trough. Then tape green construction paper on the outside of the river and on the inside of the back where kids will see it. (If the boxes came with blue liners, you're all set for water. If not, line the boxes with crumpled blue construction paper.) Finally, tape the reeds and plants in place along the front of the river. You'll find the river-making simple and fun. Just use the illustration below as your guide. When the river is complete, place a large basket in it.

Teacher Tip

The stems of artificial reeds and plants fit neatly into the corrugated rims of the produce boxes, which hold the plants firmly in place. How handy!

You'll also need to make several hand-held reeds. (Kids will hold the reeds in front of their faces as they sneak toward the river.) To make the reeds, cut sheets of green construction paper in half horizontally. Then make cuts to within an inch of the edge all along the long side of each piece of paper, so the paper resembles a comb. Then wrap each "comb" around a bath tissue tube, taping the uncut edge to the tube.

Also, cut a small, simple person shape from construction paper for each child.

Bible Adventure

For this session you'll need two helpers, one to play an Egyptian Guard and one to play Pharaoh's Daughter. Be sure the guard has a sword to add dramatic flair. Give each helper a copy of the "Finding Baby Moses" script. Cue the *Skits & Drama* CD to the "Nile River" segment (track 2).

Somewhere near the river, place a couch or table turned on its side for kids to hide behind.

Create a sense of mystery and anticipation by meeting kids in front of the closed door to your room.

Bring kids together, hold up a Bible, and

say: **Today's Bible story will show us how God cared for baby Moses, and how God cares for us. Today you're going to be actors and actresses. But before we go inside, let me ask you a question.**

ASK: • **How many of you have ever had babies in your family?**

say: **I want you to think of the name of a baby you've known. Maybe it's your brother or sister or a little cousin. If you haven't had any babies in your family, think of yourself, because you were a baby once. Think of that baby's name.** Pause. **Now that you've each got a baby's name in mind, I want to ask you another question.**

ask: • **How many of you have ever played Hide-and-Seek?**

say: **Well, today we have to do some sneaking ourselves. There's a mean guard inside this room, and he's looking for babies! You'll have to follow me inside very quietly so the guard won't hear us. And we'll need to get down on all fours until we can get to our hiding place. Ready? Here we go!**

Have one of your helpers begin the "Nile River" segment on the CD (track 2) just before you enter the room. Lead kids inside the room, cautioning them to be very quiet. Hurriedly crawl from the door to behind the couch or table you've set up as a hiding place. Motion for kids to follow you, whispering to them to keep down and to be quiet. Meanwhile, the Egyptian Guard will be pacing by the "river," probing the "reeds" with his sword and loosely following the "Finding Baby Moses" script. When everyone is in hiding, stand up and begin the Bible story. The Egyptian Guard will continue as if he doesn't hear you.

say: **Today's Bible story takes place in Egypt, where the Hebrew people have been slaves for many years. Pharaoh, the Egyptian leader, has just passed a new law that his guards should kill any Hebrew baby boy they find. In fact, Pharaoh said the guards should throw any Hebrew baby boys they find into the Nile River!** Point to the river.

ask: • **What do babies like to do a lot of the time?**

say: **Babies cry a lot, don't they? Can you imagine how awful it must have been for the Hebrew families, trying to keep their babies quiet so the guards wouldn't find them?** Tell kids to think of the babies in their families, then

ASK: • **How would you feel if someone wanted to hurt the little baby you're thinking of?**

say: **That's exactly how the family in our Bible story felt! This family had a baby boy, and his family was really scared for him. His mother and his sister, Miriam, had kept him as long as they dared, but they were afraid that the guards would find him soon. So the baby's mother decided to trust God to care for her tiny baby, and she put him in a basket in the river. Let's see what that was like.**

Set out pens, and give each person a paper baby cutout. Tell kids to each write the name of their family's baby on a paper cutout. Then explain that each person will sneak up to the river where they'll place their paper babies in the basket. Show kids how to hold the hand-held reeds in front of their faces as they sneak, and give each person a reed just before they sneak out from the hiding place. Have kids take turns sneaking from one end of the hiding place then re-entering the hiding place at the other end. Collect the reeds from kids as they return to give to the next kids ready to sneak. Remember, during this time the Egyptian guard will be following his script, searching the reeds for babies!

After kids have put their paper babies in the basket and are back in hiding,

ASK: • **What do you suppose the mother and sister did after they put the baby in the basket? What would *you* have done?**

say: **The Bible tells us that Miriam stayed near the river to see what would happen. That must have been scary, hoping no one would...Wait—I think I see someone!**

Have Pharaoh's Daughter enter. As she and the guard follow Part One of the "Finding Baby Moses" script, loudly whisper asides such as these to the kids: "Oh, no! What if Moses cries?" and "Look out, they're going to find him!" After the guard hands

Teacher Tip
You may wonder whether kids will stay quiet and get into their roles during this adventure. Will they ever! Although many kids may have heard this story before, this will be an exiting experience for everyone!

Teacher Tip
This experience is a great way to bring home the anticipation and emotion of this dramatic story without focusing on the horror of Pharaoh's cruel acts. Focus on God's care, rather than have kids dwell on Pharaoh's brutality.

the basket to Pharaoh's Daughter, your actors will freeze as you

ASK: • **What would you do right now if you were Miriam? Just look at that mean guard who could kill you and your brother with one swipe of his sword! But that's your baby brother they're holding. What would you do?** Allow kids to offer answers.

say: **Even though her knees were shaking and she was more scared than ever before in her life, Miriam walked right up to Pharaoh's daughter. C'mon—let's do what Miriam did and see what happened.** Lead kids over to your actors, then speak to Pharaoh's Daughter.

say: **My lady, would you like me to find a Hebrew woman to take care of the baby?** Wait for Pharaoh's Daughter to deliver "Finding Baby Moses" Part Two. Then the actors can leave.

say: **So Miriam took her little brother home, and Moses' mother got to take care of him until it was time for him to go live at the palace. And that's how God cared for baby Moses! Now let's see how God cares for us.**

Have kids sit in pairs or trios to answer the following questions. After each question, ask a few volunteers to share their answers with the rest of the group.

ask: • **When was a time you had something really hard to do, like Miriam did when she stood up to Pharaoh's daughter and the guard?**
 • **How did God take care of you in that situation?**
 • **What is a situation you're facing right now where you're trusting God to take care of you or someone you love?**

say: **It sounds as though we've all had times that were scary or hard and that God took care of us in those situations. The next time you face a really tough situation, remember this story of how God cared for baby Moses. Remember that God cares for us, too!**

✓ Teacher Tip

You'll be amazed at how involved in the story kids become. Writing the names of babies they know on the paper cutouts creates an instant emotional tie with the story. And holding the reeds in front of their faces gives kids that extra element to make this story really memorable.

Finding Baby Moses Script

Directions for Egyptian Guard: As kids arrive and hide, pace back and forth near the "river," probing the "reeds" with your sword. Call out, as if to other guards, using the following statements: "Keep looking for baby Hebrew boys! When you find them, throw them in the river!" and "Reinforcements! I need more guards to carry out Pharaoh's orders!" and "Keep looking! Pharaoh's orders must be carried out!"

When kids begin sneaking up to put their paper babies in the basket, move behind the river and keep calling out. Now you can add other statements, such as "Guard! Check over there—I thought I saw movement in the reeds!" and "Such a still day, and yet I see reeds moving along the Nile. There must be Hebrews nearby!"

Part One

Pharaoh's Daughter: Good morning, guard. What are you doing near the river today?

Guard: *(Bowing)* Good morning, my lady. We're searching this area for Hebrews who might be hiding their baby boys.

Pharaoh's Daughter: Well, for right now, you can guard me as I walk along the river. *(Begins walking along the river.)* Guard, what is that in the river? *(Points to the basket.)* Why, it looks like a basket! Bring it to me.

(Guard steps with one foot into the river and holds up the basket.)

Guard: Look! It's a baby! *(Hands basket to Pharaoh's Daughter.)*

Pharaoh's Daughter: *(Smiling gently)* Why, it must be one of those Hebrew baby boys! I wonder what we should do with it.

Guard: *(Laughs menacingly.)* I know what to do with this baby! *(Freezes with sword upraised.)*

Part Two

Pharaoh's Daughter: Yes, I *would* like you to find a Hebrew woman to care for the baby for a time. And I shall pay her for her trouble. Then, after a few years, I'll bring him to the palace to live with me. And I'll call him Moses, which means "I took him out of the water." *(Hands the basket to the narrator.)*

Permission to photocopy this script from *Large-As-Life Bible Adventures* granted for local church use. Copyright © Group Publishing, Inc., P.O. Box 481, Loveland, CO 80539.

Large-As-Life Bible Adventures

Bible Adventure 3

God protects the Israelites from the plagues

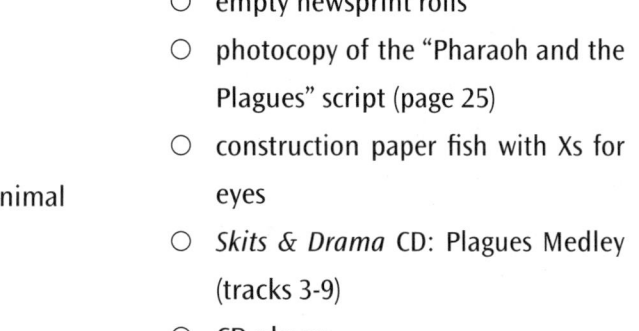

Bible Basis: Exodus 7:1–10:29

Supplies
- Bible
- clear plastic glass
- water
- spray bottle
- red powdered drink mix
- small bag of confetti
- pinch clothespins
- cardboard cow or stuffed animal
- large red dot stickers
- fly swatter
- white paper wads in a bag
- pillowcase
- chair
- box or small table
- aluminum foil
- empty newsprint rolls
- photocopy of the "Pharaoh and the Plagues" script (page 25)
- construction paper fish with Xs for eyes
- *Skits & Drama* CD: Plagues Medley (tracks 3-9)
- CD player

Preparation

Before this lesson, build "Pharaoh's throne" by simply covering a chair with lengths of aluminum foil (or a Mylar sheet). Then stand two or three empty newsprint rolls next to each side of the chair as armrests, and cover the rolls with foil, too. Place a small foil-covered table next to the throne. You'll also need a "backstage" area for your actor to retreat to during the lesson.

19

Then prepare the plagues. You'll need a spray bottle of prepared red powdered drink mix for the blood, one bag of white paper wads for the hail, a bag of pinch clothespins for the locusts, a small bag of confetti for the gnats, a cardboard cow or stuffed animal for the livestock, a package of large red dot stickers, and a pillowcase for the darkness. You'll also need "dead" construction paper fish. Kids will act out the plagues of the flies and frogs.

For this session, you'll need a male volunteer to play "Pharaoh." Choose someone with a theatrical flair, and give him a copy of the "Pharaoh and the Plagues" script (page 25) in advance. Encourage your helper to become familiar with the script. Tell him to have fun with this segment—because the kids sure will!

Place a plastic glass of water next to the throne, and place the fly swatter near the throne but out of sight. Have Pharaoh wait out of sight.

Bible Adventure

Greet kids outside the door and welcome them. Then open the door, and have kids sit on the floor.

say: **Today you're going to produce the special effects for our Bible story. In this story, the Israelites—God's special people—are slaves in Egypt. Pharaoh, the Egyptian leader, has been working the Israelites** *so hard,* **and they're** *so tired*! **Now, God has decided that it's time for his people to leave Egypt. So God called Moses, and told him to go before Pharaoh and tell him to let the Israelites go so they can worship God the way God wants them to.** Open your Bible to Exodus 7 and 8, and show kids the chapters. **The Bible tells us that Moses went before Pharaoh 10 times. Each time that Pharaoh refused to let the Israelites go, God sent a plague on the Egyptians. You may already know what a plague is—it's a horrible thing that happens to a whole land or country. Today, we're going to produce the special effects for the first nine plagues. Here's how we'll do it.**

First, we'll pretend we're Moses going before Pharaoh. Then each of you will get to inflict a plague on Pharaoh. For two of the plagues, we'll all act together. Are you ready?

say: **Moses had to go before Pharaoh, so we'll have to meet with Pharaoh, too.**

Teacher Tip

As adults, we often forget what words kids do and don't understand. It's important to explain what plague *means so everyone is on the same page.*

Here's how we'll call him: Pha-raoh! Oh, Pha-raoh! Lead kids in calling Pharaoh in a singsong voice. **Then when Pharaoh comes out, we'll say what Moses said: "Let my people go!"** Have kids practice the phrase. **Are you ready for the first plague? Let's call Pharaoh.** Lead kids in calling Pharaoh.

Pharaoh will come out, sit on the throne, and begin the "Pharaoh and the Plagues" script. After Pharaoh says "Since you're here, you might as well tell me what you want," ask kids:

- **What did Moses say to Pharaoh?**

Lead kids in shouting, "Let my people go!" As Pharaoh pretends to consider the request, choose a child or group of children to inflict the plague of blood. Have those kids come forward and each take a turn spraying the red liquid into Pharaoh's glass of water. Let kids toss the paper fish around the throne. Then have them return to their places. Pharaoh will continue with the script, then will return backstage.

say: **Pharaoh refused to let the Israelites go, so God turned all the water in Egypt to blood. All the water in the Nile River turned to blood, and all the fish died. Then God told Moses to go back and ask Pharaoh again. God said that if Pharaoh said "no," he'd send another plague—the plague of frogs!** Lead kids in calling Pharaoh. After Pharaoh responds, ask kids:

- **What did Moses say?**

Lead kids in calling out, "Let my people go!" Pharaoh will again say "no."

say: **Pharaoh still wouldn't let the people go, so God sent frogs, frogs, and more frogs. There were frogs in the streets, frogs in the houses, and even frogs in the beds. There were frogs everywhere! Let's show Pharaoh our special-effects frogs!**

Let kids hop around the throne, making *ribbit* sounds. After Pharaoh runs backstage, have kids return to their seats.

say: **The Bible says that Pharaoh's heart was hard, and he still wouldn't let the Israelites go. So God told Moses to try again. This time, if Pharaoh said "no," God would send the plague of gnats—those are tiny buzzing bugs! Let's call Pharaoh.** Lead kids in calling Pharaoh. After Pharaoh responds,

ASK: • **What did Moses say?**

Lead kids in calling, "Let my people go!"

After Pharaoh says "no,"

say: **So God sent gnats. There were gnats *everywhere*!** Pretend to swat at gnats around your head. **Let's show Pharaoh our gnats.** Choose kids to go forward, and let

Teacher Tip

Feel free to assign the plagues according to the number of kids you have. For example, if you have fewer kids, let each child do more than one plague. Or all the kids could act out more than two plagues together. How the plagues are acted out can easily be adapted to match your number of kids.

God protects the Israelites from the plagues

Teacher Tip
Your kids will have lots of fun with these plagues. And although the plagues were serious business, this experience can be an excellent way to show kids that God's power is greater than any special effects we can produce. It's also memorable and involving for everyone.

each child throw a pinch of confetti at Pharaoh. After Pharaoh runs backstage, have kids return to their seats.

say: **The Bible tells us that Pharaoh's heart was *still* hard. So God told Moses to try again. This time, if Pharaoh said "no," God would send the plague of flies! Let's call Pharaoh.** Lead kids in calling Pharaoh. After Pharaoh responds,

ASK: • **What did Moses say?**
Lead kids in calling, "Let my people go!
Pharaoh will again say "no."

say: **So God sent flies. There were so many flies you could barely see! But God only sent flies to the Egyptians. There were no flies at all where the Israelites lived! God was protecting the Israelites. Let's show Pharaoh our flies!** Lead all kids in flapping their "wings" and buzzing around the throne. After Pharaoh runs backstage, have kids return to their seats.

say: **The Bible tells us that Pharaoh said the Israelites could worship God in the desert, but they couldn't go very far. But Moses said that wasn't good enough. So God told Moses to try again. This time, if Pharaoh said "no," God would send the plague of dead livestock—livestock means horses and cows and other farm animals. Let's call Pharaoh.** Lead kids in calling Pharaoh. After Pharaoh responds,

ASK: • **What did Moses say?**
Lead kids in calling, "Let my people go!"
Pharaoh will again say "no."

say: **So God killed all of the Egyptian livestock. All of the Egyptian cattle, camels, goats, horses, sheep, and donkeys died. But *none* of the Israelite livestock died! God was protecting the Israelites. Let's show Pharaoh the Egyptian livestock.** Choose kids to come forward and hand the cardboard cow to Pharaoh. After Pharaoh runs backstage, continue.

say: **The Bible tells us that Pharaoh *still* wouldn't let the Israelites go. So God told Moses to try again. This time, if Pharaoh said "no," God would send the plague of boils!**

ask: • **Has anyone here ever had hives or a rash or mosquito bites?** Wait for a show of hands.

say: **Well, boils are like mosquito bites, only a whole lot worse. God said he would send awful sores to cover the Egyptians. But there would be no boils on the**

22   Large-As-Life Bible Adventures

Israelites, because God was protecting them. **Let's see what Pharaoh decides.** Lead kids in calling Pharaoh. After Pharaoh responds,

ASK: • **What did Moses say?**

Lead kids in calling, "Let my people go!"

Pharaoh will again say "no." When Pharaoh pretends to fall asleep, choose kids to come forward. Give each person a red dot sticker to put on Pharaoh, then have kids run back to their places. After Pharaoh returns backstage, continue.

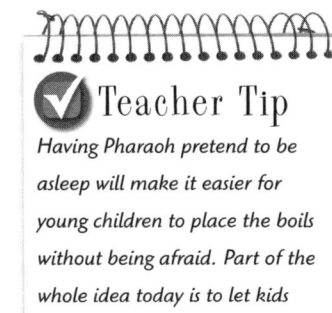

Teacher Tip
Having Pharaoh pretend to be asleep will make it easier for young children to place the boils without being afraid. Part of the whole idea today is to let kids take a non-threatening look at a potentially scary story.

say: **The Bible tells us that Pharaoh's heart was still hard, and he *still* wouldn't let the Israelites go. So God told Moses to try again. This time, if Pharaoh said "no," God warned that he would send the plague of hail! Let's call Pharaoh.**

Lead kids in calling Pharaoh. After Pharaoh responds,

ASK: • **What did Moses say?**

Lead kids in calling, "Let my people go!"

say: **So God sent hail all over the land of Egypt. The hail hammered down on all the fields of Egypt and struck every animal and person that wasn't under cover. The hail battered down and killed most of the plants the Egyptians used for food. It was the worst hailstorm ever to hit Egypt! But no hail fell on the Israelites, because God was protecting them. Let's show Pharaoh our hail!** Choose kids to come forward, and let each person throw a handful of paper wads at Pharaoh. Then have kids return to their places. After Pharaoh returns backstage, continue.

say: **The Bible tells us that Pharaoh *said* he would let the people go, but when the time came, he hardened his heart again and wouldn't let them go. So God told Moses to try again. This time God warned that, if Pharaoh said "no," he would send the plague of locusts! Let's call Pharaoh.**

Lead kids in calling Pharaoh. After Pharaoh responds,

ASK: • **What did Moses say?**

Lead kids in calling, "Let my people go!"

Pharaoh will again say "no."

say: **Pharaoh said the men could leave, but the women and children had to stay in Egypt. Moses said that wasn't good enough—God wanted Pharaoh to let *all* the Israelites go. So God sent locusts to the land of Egypt. Locusts are like grasshoppers, and they eat everything in sight! The Bible says there were so many locusts, you couldn't even see the ground! And the locusts ate what few plants were left after the hail. Let's show Pharaoh our locusts!** Choose kids to come

God protects the Israelites from the plagues

forward, and let each person pinch a clothespin on the throne. After Pharaoh goes backstage, continue.

say: **It's hard to believe, but even after the plague of locusts Pharaoh's heart was *still* hard, and he *still* wouldn't let the Israelites go. So God told Moses to try again. This time, if Pharaoh said "no," God warned that he would send the plague of darkness! Let's call Pharaoh.**

Lead kids in calling Pharaoh. After Pharaoh responds,

ASK: • **What did Moses say?**

Lead kids in calling, "Let my people go!" Pharaoh will again say "no."

say: **So God sent darkness all over Egypt. It was so dark, none of the Egyptians could see anyone else for three whole days! But where the Israelites lived, it wasn't dark at all! God was protecting the Israelites. Let's show Pharaoh our darkness.** Choose kids to come forward and drape the pillowcase over Pharaoh's head. Then, after Pharaoh returns backstage, continue.

say: **This time, Pharaoh said all the Israelites could go, but they had to leave their livestock in Egypt. Moses said that wasn't good enough. So Pharaoh told Moses to get out of his sight, because he would never let the people go. Then God sent one more plague, but that's the subject of another lesson. I'm too tired to do one more plague today!**

But we can see from today's story that God protected the Israelites, and God protects us, too. Turn to a partner and tell about a time God protected you or someone you know from something scary. Maybe you were in a bad storm, or maybe you were lost, or maybe someone you know was sick.

Give kids several minutes to discuss their protection stories, then ask volunteers to share their stories with the rest of the group.

Teacher Tip

Don't be afraid to share a personal story of your own with the kids. Sharing personal feelings and stories will make your faith real to kids and encourage them to trust God.

say: **God protected the Israelites, and God protects us! That doesn't mean that bad things won't happen to us, but it *does* mean that we can trust God through those hard times. We can always trust God to take care of us, no matter what's going on in the world around us. Just look at how God protected the Israelites. He'll protect you, too! Let's give God a cheer!** Lead kids in a "hip-hip-hooray!" cheer for God. Then close in prayer, thanking God for his protection and faithfulness.

Pharaoh and the Plagues Script

Plague #1: Blood

Pharaoh: *(Emerges from backstage and sits on the throne.)* Slaves! What are you Israelite slaves doing here in the palace? *My* palace! You're supposed to be out making bricks so I can have you build more buildings. Slaves aren't supposed to be in the royal palace! But...since you're here, you might as well tell me what you want.

*(**Kids** call out the refrain.)*

Pharaoh: *(Walking and stroking chin)* Hmmm. Let me consider your request. Let the people go. Let the people go. An interesting concept. I must consider this. *(**Kids** turn the water in the glass red.)*

*(**Sound Person** plays "Sneaking" segment (track 3).)*

Pharaoh: *(Returning to the throne, leaning back, and absently picking up the glass of water)* I've considered your request, and have come up with an answer. No!! You're slaves—plain and simple. Your parents were slaves, your children will be slaves, and I will never let you go! Got it? Good! *(Takes a sip of the red liquid, then spits and sputters.)* Blood! Yuck! My water has turned to blood! *(Runs and points to a spot in the distance.)* Look! All the water in the Nile River has turned to blood, too! And something smells! Is it you? *(Pretends to sniff a nearby child.)* No, it's not you. It's the fish! They're all dead! *(Gingerly picks up a fish and holds his nose.)* And boy, do they stink! Guards! Guards! We have a problem! *(Exits running.)*

Plague #2: Frogs

Pharaoh: *(Enters in response to **Kids'** call and sits on the throne.)* Not you again! I already gave you my answer, right before all that blood showed up. *(Shivering)* Yuck! That brings back bad memories. Look, I'm a busy man. What is it you want?

*(**Kids** call out the refrain.)*

Pharaoh: Exactly what part of "no" don't you understand? I will not let you go—not today; not tomorrow; not ever! The answer is—now listen carefully—NO!

*(**Kids** gather around the throne like frogs.)*

*(**Sound Person** plays the "Frogs" segment (track 4).)*

Pharaoh: Frogs! Frogs! I *hate* frogs! *(Dancing on tiptoes)* Get away! Get away! Help! Guards! Come here at once and he-elp me!! *(Exits running.)*

God protects the Israelites from the plagues

Plague #3: Gnats

Pharaoh: *(Enters in response to **Kids'** call and sits on the throne.)* You know, this is really getting old. I thought I got rid of you slaves once and for all yesterday. I'm running out of patience here. What do you *want*?

*(**Kids** say refrain.)*

Pharaoh: OK, OK. Here's the deal. You don't seem to be the brightest slaves in all of Egypt, so I'll say it slowly. Are you listening? Noooo. No, No, No! *(Mopping brow)* Have I made myself clear?

*(**Kids** toss confetti in **Pharaoh's** face.)*

*(**Sound Person** plays the "Gnats" segment (track 5).)*

Pharaoh: *(Pretending to swat gnats)* Gnats! Gnats! I *hate* gnats! They're in my eyes and in my nose. They're even in my mouth! *(Sputters.)* What's with you people and your God? Get out! Get out of my palace and never come back! *(Exits.)*

Plague #4: Flies

Pharaoh: *(Enters in response to **Kids'** call, sits on the throne, and shakes head slowly.)* You know, I'm really, really getting tired of seeing you slaves. Why can't you get it through your heads that I'm NOT going to let you go? Why can't you just go back to the fields and leave me alone? What do you want from me?

*(**Kids** say refrain.)*

Pharaoh: I'm telling you for the last time—you may not leave Egypt!

*(**Kids** buzz and surround the throne.)*

*(**Sound Person** plays the "Flies" segment (track 6).)*

*(**Pharaoh** pulls out the fly swatter and swings it in the air, being very careful not to hit anyone.)*

Pharaoh: Flies! Aaargh! These are worse than those gnats. I can't take any more. Get away! Get away! Go ahead—go out to the desert and worship! *(Exits.)*

Large-As-Life Bible Adventures

Plague #5: Livestock

Pharaoh: *(Enters in response to Kids' call, sits on the throne, and rubs head.)* You slaves are really getting to me, you know? I've tried to be fair. You're *slaves*—what more do you want?

(Kids say refrain.)

Pharaoh: Look. I'll say it one more time—I WILL NOT let you go. That's it! No more!

(Kids hand cardboard cow to Pharaoh.)

(Sound Person plays the "Cows" segment (track 7).)

Pharaoh: What is this? Are *all* the cows dead? And the goats? And the sheep? This is horrible! I *knew* this cow! Hey, wait a minute, is the Israelite livestock dead? No? What's going on here? Now I'll *never* let you go! *(Exits.)*

Plague #6: Boils

Pharaoh: *(Enters in response to Kids' call, sits on the throne, and puts head in hands.)* Look, this whole "Let my people go" stuff is getting me down. I know I shouldn't bother to ask, but what is it you want?

(Kids say refrain.)

Pharaoh: *(Wearily)* Let us go, let us go. That's all I ever hear. You'll have to excuse me, but I just can't deal with this anymore. It's been a rough week, you know? *(Dozing off while speaking)* You can't go, OK? Never. And no more flies, and gnats, and frogs…

(Kids apply "boils.")

(Sound Person plays the "Sneaking" segment (track 3).)

Pharaoh: *(Wakes up, looks down, and discovers boils.)* Aaack!! Boils! This is disgusting! I *hate* boils! Is there a doctor in the house? He-elp! *(Exits.)*

God protects the Israelites from the plagues

Plague #7: Hail

(**Pharaoh** *enters in response to* **Kids'** *call, sits on the throne, and points at* **Kids**.)

Pharaoh: *(Moaning)* Oh, no. How many times are you going to bother me? You're worse than those annoying gnats! Haven't you gotten the hint by now? I don't enjoy seeing you! Now what do you want?

(**Kids** *say refrain.*)

Pharaoh: *(Rolling eyes)* Read my lips: N-O. Do you know what that spells? That's right. *(Screaming)* NO! Absolutely, without-a-doubt no!

(**Kids** *throw paper hail.*)

(**Sound Person** *plays the "Hail" segment (track 8).*)

Pharaoh: OK, OK. You can go! Enough already! Just leave, would you? *(Exits.)*

Plague #8: Locusts

Pharaoh: *(Enters in response to* **Kids'** *call, sits on the throne, and shakes finger at kids.)* Look, I don't blame you for being upset. After all, I did say you could go, and then I changed my mind. But I was thinking about it, and I realized hey—you're just slaves. I'm Pharaoh! I'm the boss! So what do you little slaves want now?

(**Kids** *say refrain.*)

Pharaoh: Well, you know, I'm getting pretty sick of this whole thing. How 'bout I let the men go, but make the women and children stay here as my slaves? Nah. On second thought, I don't think you'll go for that anyway. Nope—everybody stays. No can go!

(**Sound Person** *plays the "Locusts" segment (track 9).*)

(**Kids** *attach clothespin locusts.*)

Pharaoh: *(Jumping around from foot to foot)* Oh, no! Not more bugs! These locusts are eating everything in sight! I *hate* locusts! Get them out of here! This is awful—the trees and fields are bare. Get these locusts out of here! *(Exits.)*

Plague #9: Darkness

Pharaoh: *(Enters in response to **Kids'** call, sits on the throne, and slumps.)* You people are really getting on my nerves. I've had it up to here *(gesturing toward forehead)* with these plagues! Now for the last time, what do you want?

*(**Kids** say refrain.)*

Pharaoh: Now listen to me, and listen good. I will never let you go. I don't care *what* your God does to me! The answer is NO!

*(**Kids** drape the pillowcase over **Pharaoh's** head.)*

*(**Sound Person** plays the "Sneaking" segment (track 3).)*

Pharaoh: *(Reaching out as if blind)* Hey! Who turned out the lights? I can't see a thing! *(Peeking from under the pillowcase)* Wait a minute! Why is it so dark here in Egypt? It's not dark over there where the Israelites are! I've had it! Get out of my sight, you Israelite slaves, and never come back. And the answer is still NO!

Permission to photocopy this script from *Large-As-Life Bible Adventures* granted for local church use. Copyright © Group Publishing, Inc., P.O. Box 481, Loveland, CO 80539.

Bible Adventure 4

God spares the Israelites during Passover

Bible Basis: Exodus 11:1–15:21

Supplies

Teacher Tip
If you use coffee cans to hold the paint, make sure there are no sharp edges around the rims. To be safe, cover the rims with tape.

- Bible
- newspaper
- brown paper grocery bags
- clear packing tape
- old tarps or shower curtains
- couches or other furniture
- red washable paint
- coffee cans or other paint containers with lids
- paintbrushes
- paper plates
- matzo crackers
- paper towels (both wet and dry) for cleanup
- sheer blue material
- spray bottle of water
- material squares (one per child)
- one photocopy of the "Israelite Scout" script (page 35)
- tunic and sandals for the Israelite Scout
- *Skits & Drama* CD: "Reflective Music" (track 10)
- CD player

Preparation

Before this lesson, build a simple door frame for each group of about five kids. Here's how: Stuff a paper bag with crumpled newspaper. Then fit another paper bag down over the top of the stuffed bag to form a large building block. You'll need six blocks for each door frame. To assemble one door frame, tape one block on top of another for each side of

the door. Then tape two more blocks together and tape them horizontally to the uprights to form the top of the door frame.

Before the session, lay a tarp or shower curtain on the floor where you want each "house." Then tape each door frame to its plastic flooring. (Placing the door frames at right angles to a wall allows you to tape one upright of each frame to the wall, making the structures more secure.) Then move couches or other furniture in the room near each door frame to give the feel of actual houses. Inside each house, place a handful of material squares.

Pour a little paint into each coffee can, then close the lids. Set a paintbrush at every door frame. Then prepare a paper plate of matzo crackers for each small group of kids.

For this session, you'll need a volunteer to slip into the room as you're preparing to leave "Egypt." Give your volunteer a copy of the "Israelite Scout" script (page 35) to look over. Just before the scout slips into the room, have him hang a length of sheer blue material across the doorway and mist the material with water. The material will represent the Red Sea.

Bible Adventure

Greet kids outside of the room, and welcome them. Then invite them inside, and have them sit on the floor away from the door frames.

Hold up a Bible and

say: **The Bible tells us that the Israelite people were slaves in Egypt. God wanted Pharaoh, the leader of Egypt, to let the Israelites go. So God told Moses to ask Pharaoh to let the people go. Each time that Pharaoh said "no," God sent a plague to try to convince Pharaoh to obey.**

ask: • **Does anyone know what some of those plagues were?**

say: **God sent plagues of bloody water, frogs, gnats, dead livestock, and other**

Teacher Tip

Recruit a little help for this project, and the door frames will be finished in no time! If you're making the frames outside your room, tape only two blocks together at a time to allow for easy transport.

Teacher Tip

This activity will work much better if each "house" has a feeling of privacy and intimacy. Kids will be more focused and can better understand the seriousness and magnitude of Passover. Consider setting a table next to each door frame so when kids crawl through their doorways, they'll sit under the tables. You could even drape blankets over the tables to add to the atmosphere.

Teacher Tip

Think simple! A pair of sheer curtains from a thrift store, dyed blue, works well for the Red Sea. Use packing tape to hang the curtains from the top of the doorway.

God spares the Israelites during Passover

gross stuff. Today we're going to discover what the very last plague was—and it's a biggie. This plague is very serious. God told Moses to ask Pharaoh one last time to let the Israelites go. God warned that if Pharaoh said "no," he would send the angel of death over the land at night, and all the firstborn sons in Egypt would die—from Pharaoh's firstborn son to the lowest slave's firstborn son.

But God loved the Israelites, and he said that none of their children would be harmed. God said there would be crying and wailing all over Egypt as people realized their children were dead, but in the Israelite houses, it would be so silent that not even a dog would bark. The angel of death would pass right over the houses of the Israelites. That's why it's called Passover, because the angel of death passed over the Israelites.

And God told Moses to tell the people to remember what God had done that night, and to celebrate it every year. People today, thousands of years later, still celebrate the Passover, when God passed over the Israelite houses and spared their children.

Now I know this plague sounds really terrible, but let me ask you something.

ask: • How many chances did God give Pharaoh to let the Israelites go?
• Why do you think God gave Pharaoh so many chances to obey?

say: **God gave Pharaoh plenty of chances to let the people go. Not one chance, not two chances, but lots of chances! One, two, three, four, five, six, seven, eight, and nine chances!** Count off on your fingers as you count. **And today we'll see that God gave Pharaoh one last chance. Here's what happened.**

Back in Bible times, people worshipped God by sacrificing animals to him. We don't have to do that any more, but it was the law back then. Anyway, God told Moses to tell the Israelite families to each kill a perfect lamb and roast the meat. Killing a perfect lamb was a big sacrifice—healthy lambs were worth a lot of money! If a family didn't have a lamb, they were to share with a family that did. We're going to do some sharing in just a minute.

Then they were to use the blood of the lamb to paint on their door frames to show they were Israelites. The angel of death would pass over the houses with blood painted on the door frames and would spare the children inside.

ask: • How do you think the Israelites felt when they heard what God was going to do?
• What do you suppose they were thinking as they painted blood on their door frames?

Teacher Tip

This is an awesome experience, but it requires that kids have a reflective attitude. If you have a few who struggle with being quiet and calm, rather than "shushing" throughout the activity, a gentle touch on the shoulder can help kids focus.

say: **I'll bet lots of those Israelites were praying for their families as they put blood on their door frames! We don't have a lamb to roast, but I did bring some paint that looks like blood. We're going to paint on our door frames, just as the Israelites did. We'll pretend that we're sharing houses, just as the Israelites did for their Passover meal that night so long ago. Each person can paint one or two swipes of paint on a door frame, hand the brush to the next person, and then crawl inside the house. As you paint, say a prayer out loud for each member of your family, just as the Israelites might have done. Wait quietly for your turn, and listen as others pray.**

Group kids so that each door frame has approximately the same number of kids waiting in line. Show kids how to paint on the door frame. Encourage each child to pray aloud as he or she paints, then have the child crawl through the doorway and sit quietly inside the house. As kids paint, play the "Reflective Music" segment from the *Skits & Drama* CD (track 10).

After everyone has painted and crawled inside a house, collect the paints and put lids on the containers.

say: **God also told Moses to tell the people that after the angel of death came over Egypt, they needed to be ready to leave in a hurry. People wouldn't have time to pack all their things or make a lot of food. God said people should have their coats ready to go. In your house, you'll find a head covering like the Israelites might have worn. Put it on your head so you'll be ready to go.** Pause as kids put head coverings on.

God said there wouldn't be time to cook a regular meal. He told Moses to tell the people to eat unleavened bread, which is bread that didn't have time to rise. You know, it usually takes a long time to make bread. You have to let the dough rise then wait some more. But there wasn't time for that, so the people had to eat bread that didn't rise. I have some unleavened bread for you to try.

Give each house a plate of matzo crackers . As kids eat the unleavened bread, have them answer the following questions in their "families."

ask: • **What do you think it was like eating such a strange meal?**
• **What do you think the families said to each other, knowing that this was probably the last meal they would eat in Egypt?**

say: **That night, after the Passover meal, it was dark in Egypt.** Turn out the lights. **I'll bet the children tried to stay awake, but they were probably too tired to keep their eyes open. But I'll bet that not too many of the Israelite parents slept that night.**

Teacher Tip
Painting on the door frames and praying aloud for family members can be a really powerful and solemn moment for kids. Who wouldn't be moved by hearing a young child paint a few strokes as she says, "And please protect Daddy, and Grandma, and Tiffany"?)

Teacher Tip
Whenever kids are discussing in small groups, encourage them to sit knee-to-knee so they can see their group members. This makes for easier, more meaningful communication, and gets kids to really talk face to face.

God spares the Israelites during Passover

ask: • **What do you think those parents thought as they tucked their children in bed that night?**

say: **That must have felt like the longest night in history! Can you imagine what it might have been like, knowing what was going to happen in a few hours? The night probably seemed to last forever! Let's close our eyes and wait, just as the Israelites did that night. It may seem like we're waiting a long time. But that's how they must have felt, too.** Close your eyes and wait in silence for a long minute or two. Then continue the story in a hushed voice, but with feeling.

say: **Keep your eyes closed as I tell you the rest of the story. The people waited and waited in silence for the angel of death to come over Egypt. It seemed as if they had been waiting forever. But then, right at midnight, they heard what sounded like a loud wind pass over their houses. For a short time, they heard nothing. Then, in the distance, they heard a father cry out** (pause) **and a mother scream. Soon, it seemed as though all of Egypt was filled with crying and screaming. But in the houses of the Israelites, not even a dog barked. It was just as God had promised—the angel of death had passed over their houses.**

Then, all of a sudden, an order came from Pharaoh for the Israelites to leave Egypt right away! There was no time to waste! The people knew that Pharaoh might change his mind any minute, so they had to hurry! C'mon! Hurry! Just leave your head coverings in the house. Get up! Let's go!

Motion for kids to hurry and follow you out of the room. Just as you get near the door, have the Israelite Scout stop the kids. After the scout says his lines,

ASK: • **Does anyone know how this story ends?**

say: **You'd better tell this guy how the story ends—he looks pretty scared.** If they know, let a few children tell the scout how God saved the Israelites. If kids don't know, explain that God parted the waters of the Red Sea so the Israelites could escape. Then let the scout lead children out of the room and "through" the Red Sea curtains.

Teacher Tip

You'll notice that this lesson focuses mostly on the Passover, rather than crossing the Red Sea. The Passover is a wonderful example of God's power and love, and makes a powerful connection to the story of Jesus' death and resurrection.

Israelite Scout Script

Before entering the room, hang the blue curtains that represent the Red Sea just outside the room. Mist the curtains with water from a spray bottle. Then slip quietly into the room just as the leader is urging kids to hurry out of "Egypt."

Israelite Scout: *(Breathless from running)* People of Israel, it's no use! We'll never make it out of Egypt alive! I'm a scout who's just come back, and I can tell you that Pharaoh has changed his mind again. He's getting his army together right now to chase us! And the Red Sea is right in our path—we'll never be able to get across!

*(**Kids** tell how story ends.)*

Israelite Scout: Do you really have that much faith? Does God really love us that much? I believe you! God *does* love us! C'mon! Let's cross that Red Sea!

*(**Israelite Scout** leads **kids** out of the room and through the blue curtains.)*

Permission to photocopy this script from *Large-As-Life Bible Adventures* granted for local church use. Copyright © Group Publishing, Inc., P.O. Box 481, Loveland, CO 80539.

God spares the Israelites during Passover

Bible Adventure 5

Gideon defeats the Midianites

Bible Basis: Judges 7:1-22

Supplies

- ○ assistant to operate the CD
- ○ Bible-time robe for you
- ○ 1 paper lunch sack for each child
- ○ 1 yellow glow stick for each child
- ○ leather bag to hide glow sticks
- ○ orange and yellow tissue paper for the campfire
- ○ white blinking Christmas lights for campfire
- ○ several logs to create campfire
- ○ CD player with "repeat" function
- ○ *Skits & Drama* CD: "Eve of the Battle, Part 1" (track 11) and "Eve of the Battle, Part 2" (track 12)
- ○ dropcloths or sheets
- ○ pillows, table, or sofa to make the wall

Preparation

Create a "stone wall" along one side of your room. You could lay pillows on a table (for a bumpy effect), scoot a sofa next to the table, and then drape the dropcloths or sheets over them. Make the wall big enough for the assistant to comfortably hide behind (see illustration on page 37). Set the CD player behind the wall by the assistant.

Make a no-risk, no-heat "campfire" by stacking several logs at least 15 feet from the stone wall. Stack the logs in a circle that's high enough to place a bunch of white blinking Christmas lights inside. Cover the lights with yellow and orange tissue paper.

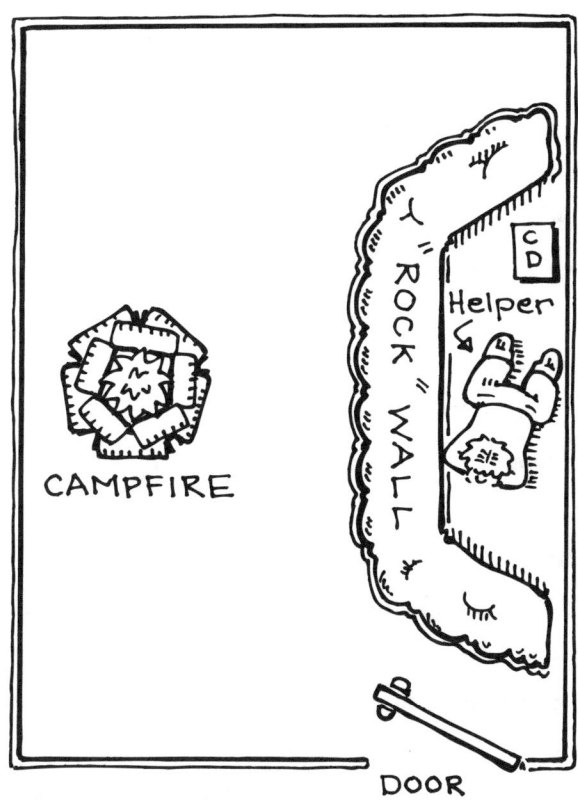

Unwrap one glow stick for each child, and place the glow sticks in a leather bag. Place the leather bag and lunch sacks by a darkened area near your campfire where kids won't see them.

Wear a simple robe so you'll look like a person from Bible times. Your assistant—who'll never be visible to the children—needn't be in costume.

Make the room as dark as possible.

Before kids enter the room, have your assistant play "Eve of the Battle, Part 1" (track 11) on the *Skits & Drama* CD, setting the CD on "repeat" so it plays the track over and over.

Teacher Tip
Your initial discussion with children takes place outside *the room. Kids will be curious about what awaits inside.*

Teacher Tip
For extra fun, place a few flashlights just below the height of the sofas and shine the lights against the wall. The lights will appear to be distant campfires, and will also provide light for the assistant.

Bible Adventure

As you meet children outside the room,

say: **Thank goodness you're here! You're the scouting party, right? Where are all the other soldiers who are coming?** Be surprised that the soldiers you were waiting for didn't come. Look around as if perhaps the rest of the army is just down the hall.

Are you telling me you're *it*? I'm supposed to beat the Midianite army and all I've got is…(count quickly and say the number of kids in your class)**…people? Boy, this day just gets better and better.**

But tell me: You *were* quiet getting here, right? Nobody saw you?

Lean in and speak confidentially. **We've got to be very quiet—the Midianite camp is just down in the valley that way. In fact, we're going to have to crawl so they don't look up and see us.**

Where we're going will be dark, but there's nothing there that will harm you. Now, there's a stone wall on the right where you'll enter—don't go near it. Head for the campfire and sit around it. Stay low as you go! And remember: Keep quiet! Shhh…

Crawl over to the campfire with the kids.

Gideon defeats the Midianites

say: **It's time for a briefing, I guess. You can hear the Midianites on the other side of that outcrop. We've got to stay over here to be safe because there are lots of them camped out in that valley—and I mean** *lots*.

I'm First-Lieutenant-Major-Colonel-Third-Class [your name], **and you're all in the army of Gideon, right? Nobody here from another army? Good.**

As the officer in charge, you want to pump up your army, so deliver the following speech with passion and gusto—but in a near whisper! **People, you're the best of the best in Gideon's army. I know that. You know that.**

When 32,000 soldiers were camped by the spring at Harod and Gideon told us anyone who was scared could go home, 22,000 soldiers left. You're part of the 10,000 who stepped up and said you'd fight. You're brave.

When Gideon took us all down to the river to get a drink of water, some of the soldiers got down on their hands and knees and lapped water like dogs. Remember? They did it like this. Show kids, and invite them to join you. **But some soldiers knelt down and brought the water up to their mouths so they could stay watchful as they drank. They did it like this.** Show kids, and invite them to join you.

Only 300 of you were watchful, and Gideon sent the other 9,700 soldiers home. You're not only brave, but you're watchful. Brave, watchful, and right now you're also…incredibly outnumbered.

The Midianites have 135,000 soldiers down there, people. That means we're outnumbered about 450 to one. But I know God. If he told Gideon it would only take 300 soldiers to win this battle, that's all we need.

They've got chariots, but we've got… *sandals*!

They've got lots of weapons, but we've got…a *positive attitude*!

They've got 135,000 trained soldiers, and we've got…well, we've got *us*!

But I know God. If he told Gideon we could take those guys, we can do it.

But maybe *you're* **not so sure. Do this: Find a partner. Sit knee-to-knee so you can talk without interruption.**

Discuss this:

• Who's someone you trust because you know the person loves you and will care for you?

Give a brief illustration from your own life. Repeat the question again, then encourage partners to discuss.

say: **While you're talking, I'll check out the Midianites!** As kids talk, take this opportunity to crawl over to the stone wall and carefully peer over the top. This is a great opportunity to quietly check in with your assistant.

Teacher Tip

Be sure to get into your role and communicate a sense of urgency and concern about being discovered by the Midianites. You're a military commander, but don't appear frightening or frightened, scary, or angry. Be playful! Your attitude will help kids enter into the imaginary world you've created in your room.

After a minute or two of discussion, call kids' attention back to yourself.

say: **Here's something I know to be true: God knows us and loves us…so we can trust him as we enter into this battle.**

Rise up on your knees and excitedly point to a distant, dark corner of the room.

say: **There it is! The signal from Gideon! It's time to get ready!**
Here are our orders:

At the same time, all 300 of us will stand up, smash a jar, blow a trumpet, and hold up a torch. All the noise will confuse the Midianites. When they hear the trumpets and see the torches, they'll think there are thousands and thousands of us up on the hills, and that we're about to attack.

Then we'll all yell, "A sword for the Lord and Gideon!"

The Midianites will panic, and maybe they'll run away.

OK, let's practice that shout—but we'll have to whisper it. Whisper it as loud as you can on the count of three. One, two, three:

"A sword for the Lord and Gideon!" Repeat three times.

Give a satisfied sigh and then look expectant as you

say: **OK, who brought the jars?**

Wait a moment as you look around and the truth seems to dawn on you. Then

say: **Nobody? Nobody remembered jars?**

Then who's got the trumpets? No trumpets? Kazoos? No kazoos either? Can anyone at least *whistle*?

How about torches? Who's got the torches? Let me guess. No torches either.

Oh, man, I'm going to get *so* busted for this…Gideon is going to send me back to cleaning up after the donkeys…

Well, let's do what we can with what we've got. Look around and pull out the stack of lunch sacks from where you hid them near the campfire.

And here's what I've got: lunch sacks—no lunch in them, but I've got the sacks. We can make some noise with lunch sacks! Do you know how to do that? I'll show you.

Demonstrate how to blow up a lunch sack and explode it with a bang as you smash it between your hands.

say: **Here's how to do it…**

1. Put two fingers in the sack and scrunch the sack around them to make a little hole, like the end of a balloon.

2. Blow up the sack and squeeze off the hole to make a paper balloon.

Gideon defeats the Midianites

3. Then hit the sack *really* hard—like this.

When the sack explodes, dive to the ground and look anxiously at the stone wall.

say: **I can't *believe* the Midianites didn't hear that. We got lucky!**

Give kids the lunch sacks, and as you do so, sternly

say: **These are military-issue lunch sacks, so be careful. You don't want them to go off too early or someone could get hurt. Don't blow them up until I tell you.**

Then pull out the glow sticks from your leather bag. Distribute the sticks, and have kids activate them by "breaking" them.

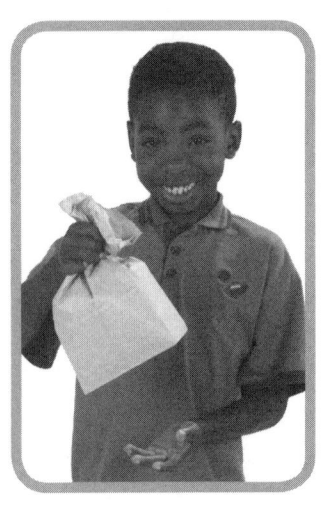

say: **Put the glow sticks on the floor after you activate them, and pick up your sacks. Now get up on your knees…put your fingers in the sack to create a paper balloon…on the count of three blow it up and seal it off. Then join me in smashing the sacks, waving the glow sticks, and shouting, "A sword for the Lord and Gideon!"**

Ready? One…two…three!

Lead children in smashing the sacks and shouting, "A sword for the Lord and Gideon!" three times. Wave the glow sticks. Your assistant will use the noise of your shouting to cover the sound of switching the CD track to the "Eve of the Battle, Part 2" (track 12) and turning up the volume.

Quickly signal kids to drop back to the ground as you peer over the wall. With great excitement report back what you see.

say: **Hey! They're so scared they're fighting *each other*! None of our soldiers is even down there! Give yourselves a cheer—we won!**

After kids cheer,

say: **Actually, we didn't do much except follow God's great plan. Let's give *God* a cheer! *He* won this battle!**

After kids cheer again, say, **Let's toss our torches down at the Midianite camp—that will give them something else to distract them!**

Lead kids in tossing their glow sticks over the stone wall. This will remove the distraction of the glow sticks, and as kids talk, your assistant can gather the glow sticks to give back to kids after class.

Ask kids to gather up the popped lunch sacks and pass them to you. This will remove distractions and eliminate the need for you to gather them later.

Ask your assistant to wait for one minute after the glow stick barrage to slowly begin turning down the volume of the "Eve of the Battle, Part 2" track so it's easier for children to hear each other and you. If the volume is decreased slowly, children won't

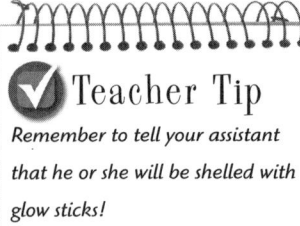

✓ Teacher Tip

Remember to tell your assistant that he or she will be shelled with glow sticks!

notice the difference.

say: **Gideon was right—we could beat the Midianites! They were so scared they fought each other. The Bible tells us that when this battle ended, the Midianites had all but wiped out each other!**

When God told Gideon to cut down his army from 32,000 to just 300, it must have sounded crazy—except Gideon knew God. Gideon knew that God would take care of his people, and that if God said just 300 soldiers could beat 135,000 enemy soldiers, that's what would happen.

And Gideon not only knew God, he acted on what God said. Gideon let people know he was a friend of God's and that he obeyed God.

Sit with a partner, knee-to-knee, and discuss this question:

• What can you say or do today that will let your family know that you know God?

Ask volunteers to share their answers with the rest of the class. Then close with a prayer, thanking God for helping us know him!

Bible Adventure 6

Elijah Confronts The Prophets of Baal

Teacher Tip

It's important to know that CO2 fire extinguishers are not the extinguishers usually found in church buildings. The standard fire extinguishers in your church will spray a messy foam! A CO2 extinguisher will spray a fog of dry ice and is most often found in labs or computer rooms. Only use a CO2 fire extinguisher! The benefits of using a CO2 extinguisher are that it will be impressively loud, put out a large cloud, and leave no residue behind.

Borrow, don't purchase, a CO2 extinguisher. It's far less expensive to recharge a canister than buy one. A small, five-pound extinguisher discharged for about 30 seconds will cost 14 dollars to recharge. It will be worth the extra cost for the extra effect!

Be sure to store the extinguisher in a safe place, away from children's reach.

Bible Basis: 1 Kings 18:1-40

Supplies

- Bible
- *Skits & Drama* CD: "Mount Carmel Mountaintop Challenge" (track 13)
- CD player with "repeat" function
- piece of paper to be your "notes"
- masking tape
- metal or sturdy plastic washtub (12-gallon size)
- gravel (available at garden centers) to half-fill the washtub
- 12 bricks (inexpensive, standard building or paving bricks)
- garden trowels or large, sturdy spoons
- 10 sticks, each about 8 inches long
- 1 large chocolate bar
- newspaper
- 3 plastic water pitchers (or half-gallon milk cartons) filled with water
- plastic siphon (available in automotive or camping stores)
- 12-inch piece of PVC pipe with a slightly bigger diameter than the siphon tube
- old bucket or empty gallon milk container
- "hammy" adult helper dressed as a firefighter
- CO2 fire extinguisher (available from fire stations or fire extinguisher providers)
- photocopy of the "Firefighter's Script" (page 47)
- cheesecloth

42

Preparation

Several days before class, recruit an adult volunteer to play the part of the firefighter, and give the volunteer a photocopy of the "Firefighter's Script" (page 47). Tell your volunteer that the script doesn't have to be memorized, but its flow should be spontaneous and natural. Ask the volunteer to wear a simple firefighter costume (a yellow slicker and a child's plastic firefighter hat will work just fine).

Before kids arrive, place a washtub on a table in your room as shown in the diagram. The tub has a section of newspaper under one end and a plastic PVC pipe at the other end; this makes it easy for water poured in the washtub to be siphoned out into a bucket or empty milk container after class. The water will drain to where the pipe is placed in the gravel, and a siphon placed down into the pipe. Place the tub at one end of the room—preferably in a corner away from plants and at least six feet from where children will be sitting. Put a masking tape line on the floor as a boundary so children know how close they can sit. For safety, you'll want children behind the line when the firefighter enters even if children are invited to gather closer while the altar is under construction.

Also, place the following items in groups around the room: bricks, sticks, pitchers of water, and garden trowels.

Set the volume of your CD player so the "Mount Carmel Mountaintop Challenge" segment (track 13) can be heard as children enter the room. Set your CD player to "repeat" so the track repeats until you turn it off.

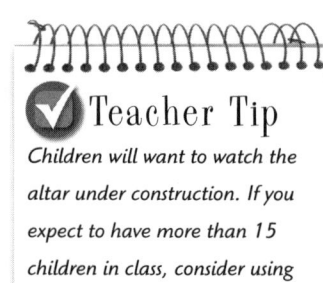

Teacher Tip

Children will want to watch the altar under construction. If you expect to have more than 15 children in class, consider using a small plastic swimming pool rather than a washtub as a base for your altar construction.

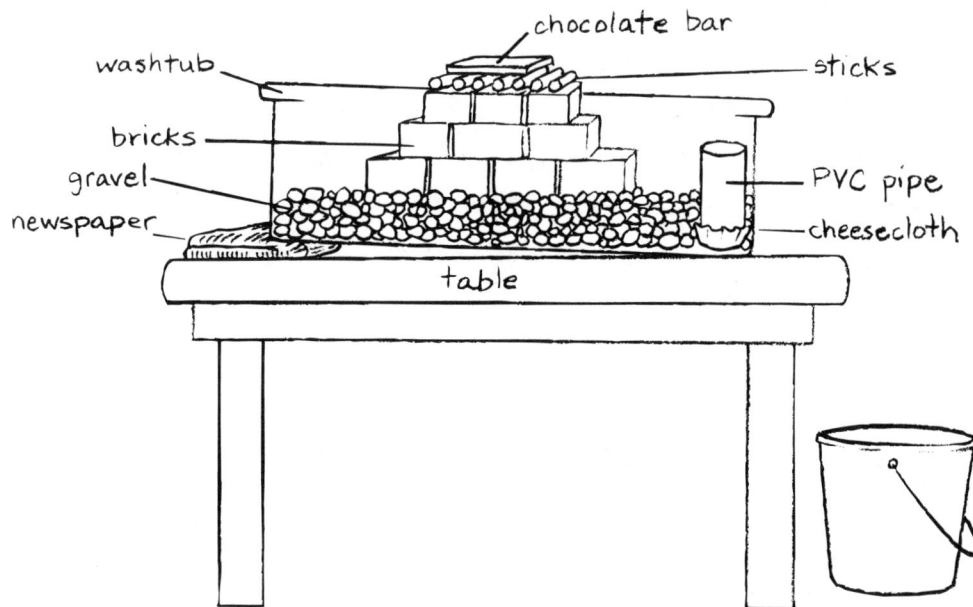

Elijah Confronts The Prophets of Baal   43

Bible Adventure

As kids gather by the door to your room, greet them excitedly.

When you're ready to begin,

say: **I'm glad you all finally got here! It's halftime at the Mount Carmel showdown! You missed the first half of the game, but you're just in time for the second half—and you're going to join one of the teams. We'll be climbing to the top of a tall mountain called Mount Carmel, so stick together.**

As you walk into the room, lean over as if you're struggling uphill, and encourage kids to watch out for bears. Then ask kids to form small groups of about four or five and sit in circles on the floor.

Hold up your opened Bible and

say: **We made it! Today we're back in Old Testament times here in our Bible adventure. That means we're way back before Jesus came to the earth and was born in Bethlehem. There are people around who believe in God, and one of them is a prophet named Elijah.**

Prophets are people who hear God's voice and tell people what God has to say. Sometimes people don't want to hear God's messages, and that gets prophets in trouble. That's what happened to Elijah. He told King Ahab that God wasn't happy because Ahab was following a false god instead of the one true God. In fact, Elijah challenged the prophets who worshipped the false god to a showdown on top of a mountain called Mount Carmel.

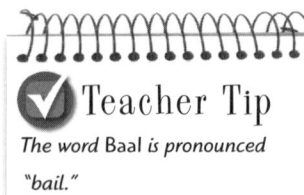

The word Baal is pronounced "bail."

Here's what happened earlier today: The 450 prophets of Baal—that's the false god—built an altar. They piled up rocks to make a table. Then they killed a bull as a sacrifice and laid it on top of a big pile of wood on the altar.

Elijah's challenge was that if Baal sent fire from heaven to burn up the sacrifice, it would prove Baal was the true God. But if Elijah's God sent fire from heaven to burn up a sacrifice, it would prove Elijah's God was real. You see, Elijah wanted people to believe in God!

All morning the 450 prophets of Baal danced around and shouted at Baal to send down fire, and you know what happened? Nothing! No fire! That's because Baal isn't real.

Now it's *Elijah's* turn, and we're going to help. Point to your notes. **Elijah gave us directions on how to prepare a sacrifice.**

We've got to build an altar on this gravel. Let's start with bricks. They'll be our stones. Elijah built an altar out of 12 stones—one stone for each tribe of Israel. If

Large-As-Life Bible Adventures

you're wearing the most green in your group, please go get two bricks and bring them up here. You may have to carry one brick at a time. (If you have fewer than six groups, kids may need to carry more bricks.)

Help the "green" volunteers quickly create a multilevel brick platform. Refer to your notes.

say: **Now we need to dig a trench—that's a ditch—around the brick platform. If you're wearing the most red, please grab a trenching tool and get to it.**

Help the "red" volunteers quickly create a shallow trench in the gravel. Refer to your notes.

say: **Now we need to put some wood on our brick altar. If you're wearing the most blue, please get some sticks and put them on the altar.**

Help the "blue" volunteers quickly stack sticks on the bricks for the "fire." Refer to your notes.

Teacher Tip

It really doesn't matter how you differentiate between group members. You could have kids number off if you choose. Just be sure that each child gets a chance to contribute to building the altar.

say: **Now it's time to place the sacrifice on the altar.**

Step to one side to indicate you're stepping out of character.

say: **We're not *really* in Old Testament times, so we're not going to do this exactly like Elijah did it. Instead of cutting up a bull for a sacrifice, we're going to sacrifice this** (hold up the wrapped candy bar)**—a chocolate bar. In Elijah's day a bull was very valuable, even more valuable than a delicious, mouth-watering chocolate bar is to us today. If you're wearing the most brown, please come on up and carefully unwrap this chocolate bar. Then place it on the altar.**

Step back in character, and help children quickly unwrap the chocolate bar and place it on the altar.

Teacher Tip

The candy bar will be sure to get a reaction from the kids! They will instantly connect to the idea of a sacrifice and might beg you not to waste the chocolate. It's a wonderful way to help them understand that building an altar involved giving up something valuable for God.

say: **Guess we're ready now to ask God to call down fire, so you'd better scoot back behind the line.** Refer to your notes. **No…wait…Elijah asked us to do one more thing—pour water on the sacrifice. Those of you wearing the most white in your group, please bring up one of the pitchers of water and pour it on the chocolate. When we want to set sticks on fire, we don't pour water on them! Why would Elijah want to do it?** Let children respond. **When God sets the sacrifice on fire, he wants everyone to know that only God could have done it! Elijah wants people to believe in God!**

Help children quickly pour a pitcher of water on the chocolate and wood. Thank them, and refer to your notes as they're heading back to their groups.

Teacher Tip

Be sure to stick to the script for this lesson, since it's designed to let each person in each group have an important role in building the altar. This is an awesome way to get every group member actively involved in the Bible story. No one is left out…or can tune out!

say: **Wait a minute—Elijah wants us to pour water *again* on the sacrifice. Come** on back and pour another pitcher of water on it.

Thank kids again when they've finished, and send them back to their groups. Refer to your notes, and quickly stop them again.

say: **Sorry—but I checked the list again. Elijah wants us to pour water on the sacrifice *three* times. Get that last pitcher.**

As kids add the third pitcher of water, comment about how if God can light a sacrifice on fire after it's soaked in water that he would certainly help people believe in him.

Check your list again, and then send the kids back to sit with their groups.

say: **Here's what happened next…**

At that cue, your firefighter accomplice will noisily burst into the room!

say: **Our firefighter friend was right: When Elijah prayed over *his* sacrifice, something *amazing* happened.**

All morning the prophets who served Baal had prayed and screamed and danced and did everything they could to get the attention of their god. And nothing happened because Baal was a made-up god. He wasn't real.

But Elijah prayed, "Lord, let people know that you are God in Israel and that I'm your servant. Help turn the hearts of the people back to you."

And fire *fell* from the sky. It consumed the pieces of meat. The wood disappeared in a flash of heat. The 12 stones disappeared in the fire. Even the mountaintop was scorched, and the water in the trench was licked up.

And the people who were watching fell on their faces crying, "The Lord—he is God! The Lord—he is God!" They believed because they saw the power of God!

Ask groups to circle up closely, knee to knee, and discuss the following questions. After each question, invite groups to share their answers with the rest of the class.

ASK: • **If you'd been on Mount Carmel when the fire fell and burned up Elijah's altar, how would you have felt? What would you have said?**

• **What do you believe about God? Why?**

• **If you could ask God any question, what would it be?**

• **What's one thing that's different about the way you live because you believe in God?**

say: **Elijah wanted people to believe in and follow God. That's what I want for all of you, too. I want you to believe in God!**

But maybe you *don't* believe in God. Or maybe you haven't heard enough about Jesus to decide if you believe yet.

Teacher Tip

Don't cue your firefighter to enter the room until every child is back behind your safety line. Safety first!

Teacher Tip

Even though your firefighter may be dressed in an inexpensive—and almost silly-looking—costume, he definitely will surprise the kids. It's a simple way to bring in some of the drama and excitement of that day on Mount Carmel.

Teacher Tip

Forming knee-to-knee circles for discussion makes such a difference, allowing kids to make eye contact, hear each other, and tune in to important life-application discussions. So don't be afraid to remind kids to huddle up close!

God wants faith that starts in our hearts and then comes out of our mouths. *Saying* you believe doesn't mean much if you don't *really* believe with your heart.

I want you to know that it's always OK to talk with me about God and Jesus and to ask any question you have. This is a safe place to have questions and to ask them.

Thanks for having fun during our Bible adventure today. Thanks for learning about God with me!

Teacher Tip

The questions you'll ask today are designed to not only review the Bible story but to also give you insight into the spiritual condition of children in your class. Don't assume they all believe in God or that what they believe is necessarily accurate!

What you learn as you thoughtfully listen to children's answers will help you know how to best serve and minister to your children in weeks to come.

FIREFIGHTER'S SCRIPT

Firefighter: Everyone stay seated! Everyone stay calm! *(Discharge a brief blast from a CO2 fire extinguisher at and over the altar. Be sure not to aim your extinguisher at anyone. After discharging the canister, remove any helmet you might be wearing.)*

Leader: What are you *doing*? You scared us half to death!

Firefighter: You can't be too careful about these things—you know what happened the last time someone built an altar like that?

Leader: You mean when Elijah did it?

Firefighter: Yeah. Elijah prayed and fire fell and burned up the sacrifice. And the wood. *And* the stones. Can't have that happening here—too many kids around.

Leader: We'll be careful.

Firefighter: Make sure you are. Remember kids: Only you can fight forest fires! Stop, drop, and roll. Bye-bye.

(Quickly exit.)

Permission to photocopy this script from Group's *Large-As-Life Bible Adventures* granted for local church use. Copyright © Group Publishing, Inc., P.O. Box 481, Loveland, CO 80539.

Bible Adventure

Jonah Disobeys God

Bible Basis: Jonah 1–3

Supplies

- Bible
- large box fan
- clear wide packing tape or duct tape
- 2 10x25-foot rolls of black plastic
- 2 cans of tuna in an open plastic container
- 10-inch lengths of braided twine (1 per participant)
- *Skits & Drama* CD: "Undersea Sounds" (track 14)
- CD player with repeat function
- photocopy of the "Special-Effects Assistant Tip Sheet" (page 53)

Teacher Tip

Before children arrive, set the volume of your CD player loud enough so the "Undersea Sounds" track can be heard inside the "fish" while the fan is on. Also be sure the light outside the fish will let enough light in near the fan so you can see this book. Place the tuna in an open plastic container or bowl that won't tip over easily and will allow the smell to waft through the inside of the plastic fish. Mmm! (Tuna is also available in plastic packets, which also works well.)

Preparation

Before kids arrive, use a box fan, clear wide packing tape or duct tape, and sheets of black plastic to make a giant "fish." Here's how!

How to Create a Big Fish!

• Lay the two sheets of black plastic side by side on the floor, and tape them together.

• With one person at each end, gather the plastic so the 20-foot width is reduced to about 10 feet.

• Tape both long edges to the floor.

- Put a large box fan just under one end of the plastic so the breeze from the fan will blow in. Put the seam between the two sheets of plastic on the top center of the fan, and tape it down around the fan.

- Gather the remaining width of the plastic, and tape it to the floor on both sides of the fan.

- At the open end, gather (make pleats) and tape the plastic to the floor.

- At that same end (opposite the fan), cut about a 6-foot opening in the center seam. This will serve as the "door" or "mouth" of the fish.

- Turn the fan on high or medium to inflate the fish. When it's almost completely inflated, turn the fan to medium or low. (If you leave the fan on high, you'll end up with a flying fish!)

- And if you want to ensure you'll have light inside to see your notes, cut a small "window" out of the black plastic and cover the opening with clear packing tape. This way, you won't need to juggle a flashlight in order to see your script.

Also, give your helper a copy of the "Special-Effects Assistant Tip Sheet" (page 53). Take the time to run through the lesson with your assistant so he or she can practice.

Bible Adventure

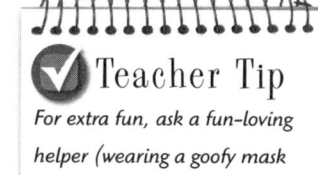

Teacher Tip
For extra fun, ask a fun-loving helper (wearing a goofy mask and snorkel) to greet children and escort them to the fish. That way you can be inside the fish to welcome children and direct them where to sit.

As kids gather by the door to your room, greet them warmly. Wear a pair of goggles if possible for fun and effect.

When the whole group has gathered by the door and you're ready to begin, hold up your opened Bible and

say: Today we'll dive into a fun Bible story—and I mean *dive*. That's because some of our story takes place underwater. Let's take deep breaths and then hold them as we dive into our Bible adventure. Show me your best underwater swimming strokes as you go!

Lead kids into the room and over to the opening of the plastic fish.

say: Oh no! A giant fish has appeared and it's going to swallow us all! Well, there's no point in swimming against the tide, as they say. Let's jump in and find a place to sit without touching the walls. Here we go!

Jonah Disobeys God

Teacher Tip

Kids are likely to be very excited when they land inside the giant fish. Be sure to take an attention-getting signal with you into the fish so you can quickly regain their attention and continue the story. Telling the second part of the story in a hushed voice is another good way to encourage kids to listen carefully.

Teacher Tip

The "live" sound effects from your assistant are so important to this story! The CD sound effects will be fun...but kids won't expect these "real" sounds to come from outside the fish!

After children are inside, start the *Skits & Drama* CD: "Undersea Sounds" (track 14), and set your CD player on "repeat" so the track will continue while you're in the plastic fish.

Be sure you're seated next to the fan so that curious children won't block the airflow and cause the fish to deflate.

Open your Bible to Jonah 1, and show it to the kids.

say: **Our story today is also about a prophet. A prophet is someone who hears a message from God and who passes that message along to other people. But the prophet we'll talk about today absolutely** *didn't* **want to obey God. The prophet's name was Jonah, and he was** *disobedient.* **You can read his story in the Bible, in the book of Jonah.**

By the way, when I say "story" please don't think that what I'm about to tell you is a made-up story like "Pinocchio" or "Jack and the Beanstalk." This story is about something that really happened.

Jonah was so disobedient that when God told him to go *this* **way** (point right) **he went** *that* **way** (point left). **Let's practice something. As you listen to Jonah's story today, every time you hear that Jonah was disobedient, point your left thumb to the left and say, "Wrong way, Jonah."**

Have kids practice that response several times before continuing.

say: **Long ago God told Jonah, "Jonah, go to the city of Nineveh. The people in that city are so bad that I might have to destroy them. Tell them to pray to me and change their ways!"**

Jonah thought, "God wants me to go to Nineveh, but I'm not going." Pause and have kids say, "Wrong way, Jonah." **"Those people from Nineveh are my country's enemies! I** *want* **God to destroy them!"**

So instead of starting out for Nineveh, Jonah ran down to the boat dock, bought a ticket, and got on a boat that was going the opposite direction from Nineveh. Pause and have kids say, "Wrong way, Jonah."

Once Jonah was on the ship, he went down below deck and found a nice place to hide and take a nap.

Was Jonah supposed to be sleeping? No—he was supposed to be going to Nineveh! Jonah wasn't obeying! Pause and have kids say, "Wrong way, Jonah."

But God knew where Jonah was. God sent a howling storm to stop the ship. (Assistant will jostle the plastic of the fish.) **The wind blew.** (Assistant will make the sounds of wind.) **The waves crashed into the ship.** (Assistant will hit the sides of the fish to make crashing wave sounds.) **The sailors were so afraid that the captain woke**

Jonah up. *(Assistant should keep making the storm sounds.)*

Shake a child sitting next to you.

say: **The captain shouted, "Get up and pray to your God to stop this storm before we all die!"**

Jonah knew God had sent the storm. Jonah said, "The only way to stop this storm is to throw me into the sea."

So the sailors picked up Jonah and tossed him into the water. And immediately the storm stopped! *(Assistant will stop his or her sound effects.)*

Was Jonah supposed to be in the ocean? No—he was supposed to be going to Nineveh! Pause and have kids say, "Wrong way, Jonah."

In a hushed voice,

say: **Down Jonah went into the dark water. A huge mouth opened right before his eyes, and faster than you can say "fish bait!" he was swallowed up by a huge fish!** Open your arms like a huge mouth, then pull them shut. **Jonah lay in the dark. He could smell fish. And he could hear the sounds you hear inside a fish. He heard the heartbeat** *(assistant will start thumping a heartbeat rhythm on the outside of the fish)*, **and he heard the fish's stomach growling** *(assistant will make the sounds of a growling, grumbly fish belly!)* **as the fish started to digest what was in his tummy—and that was Jonah! Jonah was in trouble!**

"Poor me!" Jonah said. "I should have gone to Nineveh as God said. I should have obeyed God!"

Then Jonah remembered that God is loving and kind.

So Jonah prayed, "O Lord, I promise to obey you and do whatever you ask. Amen."

That prayer sounds familiar to me because I have to pray it sometimes, too. Sometimes I know what's the right thing to do, but I don't do it. Or I know that something's wrong, but I do it anyway. I'm like Jonah—I don't always obey. And I'll bet you don't always obey either.

But just like Jonah, we can ask God for forgiveness.

Wait—something's happening! The fish's heartbeat is faster *(assistant will make the heartbeat sounds more quickly)*. **The fish is swimming somewhere…and I can hear waves in the background** *(assistant will make the sound of crashing waves)*. **We must be heading to shore.**

That's what happened—the great fish swam right up on the shore and urped out Jonah, right onto the beach *(assistant will make "urping" sounds, with as much decorum as possible!)*.

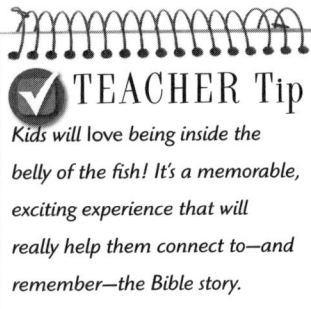

TEACHER Tip

Kids will *love being inside the belly of the fish! It's a memorable, exciting experience that will really help them connect to—and remember—the Bible story.*

That means it's time for you all to get urped! Let's get out of here!

Have kids form pairs, and give each person a length of twine.

say: **I don't know what Jonah did first. Maybe he prayed and thanked God. Or maybe he took a shower! But I know what Jonah did very soon: He went to Nineveh.**

Jonah told the people in Nineveh they needed to quit doing bad things. They needed to follow and honor God or God would destroy their city. And the people listened and changed, so God spared their city.

You know, when we caught Jonah disobeying God we pointed our left thumbs to the left and said, "Wrong way, Jonah!"

I don't want to be a Wrong-Way Jonah—I want to be a Right-Way [insert your name]. **I want to obey God! I'd like each of you to remember to obey God by loosely tying your piece of twine to your right wrist or ankle. You'll have just 60 seconds to make your bracelets, so work together with your partner to accomplish that task.**

Give a 30-, 20-, and 10-second countdown so partners know how quickly they have to work. When 60 seconds have passed, ask everyone to raise his or her right hand.

Then discuss the following questions. After each question, invite volunteers to share their answers with the rest of the group.

ask: • **How did you feel when you went into the fish? How was that like the way Jonah felt when he knew he'd disobeyed God?**

• **What did Jonah learn?**

• **What's a rule that's really hard for you to obey at home or school? Why?**

• **What's something God has asked you to do that's hard to obey? Why?**

say: **Jonah's problem wasn't figuring out what to do. God told him what to do. Jonah's problem was obeying God. I'm like that sometimes, too. I know the right thing to do, but I don't do it. Or I know what I'm not supposed to do, but I do it anyway. I don't obey. I'll bet you're like that sometimes, too.**

For the rest of today, let's let our bracelets remind us not to be Wrong-Way Jonahs. Instead, let's obey God and go God's way!

Special-Effects Assistant Tip Sheet

- When Jonah goes beneath the deck, rap your fists on a tabletop to make the sound of footsteps.

- When Jonah is sleeping, snore loudly several times.

- When the storm arises, begin by making a "whoosh" sound, then grab hold of the top of the plastic fish and gently shake it, making storm sounds.

- When the sailors toss Jonah into the water, yell "ahh!" and follow it with a loud "sploosh!" Then abruptly stop the storm sounds.

- When the narrator talks about the fish's heartbeat, pat the plastic in a heartbeat rhythm. Make growling noises to sound like a fish tummy.

- When the narrator talks about the fish swimming, increase the heart rate. Make wave "swoosh" sounds as the fish nears shore.

- When the fish "urps" Jonah onto the beach, let loose with what sounds like a huge, extended belch.

- Be on hand to help steady children as they exit the fish.

Permission to photocopy this handout from *Large-As-Life Bible Adventures* granted for local church use. Copyright © Group Publishing, Inc., P.O. Box 481, Loveland, CO 80539.

Bible Adventure 8

Jesus calms a storm

Bible Basis: Matthew 8:23-27

Supplies

- Bible
- CD player
- Life Savers candies (1 per child)
- 2 box fans
- extension cords so you can position the fans
- helper to turn a fan on and off
- 2 spray bottles carefully cleaned and filled with water
- life ring or life jacket
- *Skits & Drama* CD: "Scared at Sea" (track 15) and "We Can Trust Jesus" (track 16)
- photocopy of the "Official Fan Club Cue Card" (page 58)

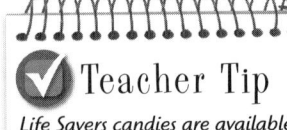

Teacher Tip

Life Savers candies are available by the bag in individually wrapped packages. You can save time by using individually wrapped Life Savers for this activity. If you purchase Life Savers in rolls, plan to unwrap them ahead of time and store them in a resealable bag.

Preparation

Before kids arrive, set box fans on both sides of your storytelling area aiming slightly up so they'll blow directly over the kids. You may need to readjust the direction of the fans depending on where kids sit, so allow for adjustments. Set a spray bottle of water beside each fan. Cue the *Skits & Drama* CD to "Scared at Sea" (track 15).

Give your helper a copy of the "Official Fan Club Cue Card" (page 58), and ask your helper to stand near one fan. You'll operate the other fan during the instant Bible drama.

Bible Adventure

When the children are all gathered by the door,

say: **Welcome! Are you ready for a Bible adventure?** Huddle children around you, and say in a hushed voice: **I sense rough seas ahead, so let's stay close together. Let's gather quickly in our story area. There are dark clouds on the horizon, and we don't want to get caught in a storm at sea.**

Lead the children into your room and weave a bit from side to side as you exclaim that the waves are high. Have kids sit close together on the floor between the two fans.

Open your Bible to Matthew 8, and show it to the kids.

say: **Today's Bible story is found in the book of Matthew, chapter 8. The book of Matthew is great because it's all about what Jesus did, who he hung out with, and what people learned from him.**

Today is all about a day in Jesus' life. The day started in a little town next to the Sea of Galilee. A lot of Jesus' disciples grew up around the Sea of Galilee; some of Jesus' disciples—like Peter, James, and John—had worked as fishermen. They knew all about how dangerous it was to be on the water in a little boat when a storm came up.

On this particular day Jesus had spent hours teaching people about God and healing sick people. You see, sometimes when people were sick, they came to Jesus because they knew Jesus was powerful. They knew Jesus could heal them. These were people who trusted God.

By the end of the day, Jesus was exhausted.

Now we'll find out what happened next, and we'll find out by being in a play. Don't worry, there aren't any lines to learn—but you each have a role in the play!

Everyone, I need you to scoot around so you're lined up shoulder to shoulder to each other. Make several lines, facing me, as if you're sitting in a row of

Jesus calms a storm

chairs. **Now scoot close together so you can put your arms around the shoulders of the people next to you. If you're at the end of a line, you'll have your arm around just one person.** Pause as kids get situated. If you have adult or teen volunteers in your classroom, position them in the middle of each row.

When everyone is in position, select a confident, dramatic child to play the part of Jesus. Position "Jesus" at the front of the room next to you, facing the children.

Teacher Tip
If you're looking for a place to involve your children's ministry director, pastor, or other church leader, you might consider using that person as "Jesus" in today's Bible drama.

say: **You're all playing the part of the disciples in our play. You need to stay seated, hang on to your fellow disciples, and remain quiet as you play your parts. Listen closely to hear what you're supposed to do. I'll start the soundtrack for our play now. Jesus, you'll have some actions to do, too, so get ready.**

Start the *Skits & Drama* CD, track 15: "Scared at Sea."

After the instant drama, lead kids in giving themselves a hand.

Then have kids form pairs to discuss the following questions. After each question, invite partners to share their answers with the rest of the class.

ask: • **What's the biggest storm you've ever seen? How did you feel?**

• **Who is a person you trust? Why do you trust this person?**

• **Do you think God can be trusted? Why or why not?**

• **How does it feel knowing the same Jesus who could calm waves and wind cares for you, too?**

say: **Sometimes I'm a little jealous of the disciples. True, they were in a terrible storm. But they got to see Jesus instantly calm the waves and wind. That helped them trust God because they'd seen Jesus' power.**

Jesus isn't here in the flesh to do that today, but he knew *you'd* be here. And he knew you'd need to trust him, too. So Jesus made sure that in the Bible there are words that will help us know he loves us, knows us, and that we can trust him.

Let's listen to some things Jesus said and some promises God has placed in the Bible.

Give kids 10 seconds to sit or lie someplace comfortable. Ask children to close their eyes.

say: **Listen very quietly to these words from the Bible. God can talk to us through the Bible. Let the Word of God calm your heart just as Jesus' words calmed the storm.**

Play the "We Can Trust Jesus" segment (track 16) from the *Skits & Drama* CD.

At the end of the segment, stop the CD, and ask kids to remain quietly in their places.

Hold up a lifesaver ring or life jacket.

say: **When the disciples were afraid their boat would sink, they must have wished they had lifesavers like this one to keep them safe. Lifesavers help us feel safe because we trust them to keep our heads out of the water if we fall into deep water. We have a lifesaver we can trust when it feels like we're in trouble, too: Jesus. I'll remind each of you that you have a trustworthy lifesaver by sharing a Life Savers candy with you today.**

Before I pass out the candy, please pray with me. Thank God for loving the children and for being our lifesaver. Ask for God to be in the heart and life of each child.

When you've finished praying, say, "[Child's name], trust Jesus as your lifesaver" as you hand a candy to that child.

When all kids have received their candy,

say: **As you enjoy your candy treat, remember that you also have a lifesaver: Jesus!**

Jesus calms a storm

Official Fan Club Cue Card

When the narrator says,

"The wind is beginning to blow,"

turn your fan on low.

When the narrator says,

"And now the wind is growing strong,"

turn your fan on medium.

When the narrator says,

"And now the wind is tearing into the boat,"

turn your fan on high.

When the narrator says,

"Waves are crashing over the sides of the boat!"

spray water into the breeze from the fan
(*not* into the fan!).

When the narrator says,

"He's telling the storm to stop,"

turn off the fan.

Permission to photocopy this handout from Group's *Large-As-Life Bible Adventures* granted for local church use. Copyright © Group Publishing, Inc., P.O. Box 481, Loveland, CO 80539.

Bible Adventure 9

Peter walks to Jesus on the Sea of Galilee

Bible Basis: Matthew 14:22-33

Supplies

- Bible
- CD player
- flashlight
- penlight
- large cardboard pieces (such as appliance boxes) or long tables
- air mattresses, inner tubes, and/or old sofa cushions and pillows
- a large box fan
- clear packing tape
- 10x25-foot piece of black plastic
- *Skits & Drama* CD: "Disciples at Sea" (track 17)
- large plastic garbage bags

Teacher Tip

Begin collecting air mattresses and inner tubes several weeks before this session. Test the inflatables to ensure they hold air. Determine how many you'll need to form a "sea" along one side of your room.

Preparation

Before this session, choose a dark side of your room to create the "sea." The sea should be about 6 feet wide, along one wall. Clear chairs and tables from your room; then build the sea on one side of your room. The sea consists of "waves" made of inflated air mattresses and inner tubes placed together. You can also use old sofa cushions (youth group areas often have these) and pillows along with the inflatables. You'll find the sea-making simple and fun. Lay the inflatable items on the floor, and use packing tape to hold them together. Place cushions and pillows randomly next to or on top of the mattresses to create the look of a rough sea. Then lay black plastic on top to complete your sea.

After you build your sea, create a "boat" at one end of the sea. (Kids will climb out of the boat and walk across the sea during the Bible adventure.) You could turn long tables on their sides and have kids gather behind them or create a simple boat using large cardboard appliance boxes. (Simply cut the appliance box down the middle, from top to bottom, and you'll have two easy boats!) Another option is to use the cushionless sofas, or you could even make a masking tape outline of a boat.

Next, place a fan away from the sea and pointing toward it. Darken the room by taping black plastic or large plastic garbage bags over the windows, if necessary. (Black plastic is available at most discount or hardware stores.)

For this session you'll need one helper who will shine a flashlight on you and play the "Disciples at Sea" segment (track 17) of the *Skits & Drama* CD. Be sure your helper listens to the segment ahead of time so he or she will be familiar with it. This helper can also operate the fan at your prompting.

Bible Adventure

Create a sense of mystery and anticipation by meeting kids in front of the closed door to your room.

Bring kids together in a huddle, and

say: **I'm glad you're here! I'm warning you right now that what happens in this cave may not be like any kind of Bible adventure you've ever experienced before! I hope you're all ready. You never can tell what may happen once we enter this room!**

Open your Bible to Matthew 14:22-33, and show kids the passage.

say: **Today's story is about Peter and an unusual thing that happened to him one night.**

We're going to travel back in time nearly 2,000 years. Line up with your hands on the shoulders of the person in front of you. When everyone's connected, we'll be ready to enter our time-travel cave. Close your eyes and depend on me to guide you safely. Whisper: **Time travel also requires perfect silence. We wouldn't want to end up in the wrong century, so everyone must be perfectly quiet. It's very dark**

where we're going, so walk carefully. Here we go!

Open the door just far enough for kids to squeeze through. Have your helper shine the flashlight on the floor as you guide the kids into the boats and invite them to sit down. When everyone has entered the room, have your helper shine a penlight on you as you sit down and begin to tell the story.

say: **Here we are in a boat—at night!**

ASK: • **How many of you have ever been in a boat?**
• **What was it like?**
• **How many of you have been in a boat at night?**
• **How was that different?**

If no one has been in a boat at night,

ASK: • **What do you think it would be like to be in a boat at night? Why?**

say: **Our Bible story is about Peter and the rest of Jesus' disciples being in a boat late at night on the Sea of Galilee.**

Play the "Disciples at Sea" segment (track 17) of the *Skits & Drama* CD fairly loudly as you begin to tell the story. Have your helper turn on the box fan.

say: **After a busy day feeding over 5,000 people, Jesus needed some time to pray. So he sent his friends out in a boat on the Sea of Galilee. The Sea of Galilee is a huge lake, and the disciples were way out on the lake, far away from land. It was dark, and the wind started to blow hard.**

ask: • **How do you think it would feel to be on that boat?**

say: **Well, by now it was very late at night, and the disciples were tired. The wind was blowing, making the boat rock back and forth. As they tried to steady the boat, the disciples looked out on the water. Something was walking—on the water! No, it couldn't be! It looked like a...well, could it be? Out on that wavy, windy sea, the disciples thought they saw—a ghost! And they thought the ghost was walking on top of the water—toward them!**

ask: • **How do you think the disciples felt now?**

say: **The disciples were so afraid! Then the ghost—or whatever it was—called out to them. It sounded just like Jesus! Could it really *be* Jesus?**

ask: • **What do you think you would've done if you had been in the disciples' boat?**

Teacher Tip
Point the penlight at the kids responding. That way they know it's their turn to respond. You may want to cover the light somewhat with your hand so you won't blind kids when you point the light at them!

Teacher Tip
In order to be heard over the noise of the CD and fan, you'll have to tell the story loudly! This atmosphere will really set the stage—after all, it probably was noisy out on a stormy sea! It's a great way to help kids experience the Bible in a more realistic way.

Peter walks to Jesus on the Sea of Galilee

say: **You won't believe what happened next! Jesus told the disciples to be brave, and then Peter spoke up. Peter said, "Lord, if it's you, tell me to come to you on the water." And Jesus said, "Come." So Peter got out of the boat and started walking on top of the water! Let's see what that might have been like for Peter.**

Guide the kids onto the air mattress "sea" and have them practice walking on the "water."

ask: • **How does it feel to be walking on our pretend sea?**
• **How do you think Peter felt walking on real water?**

say: **Peter walked a little way toward Jesus, but then he noticed the waves and felt the wind blowing. Peter got scared.**

ask: • **Why do you think Peter was afraid?**
• **Why do you suppose Peter wasn't afraid at first?**
• **When did you have courage to do something scary?**

say: **Peter's fear caused him to start sinking into the water.** Have kids drop to their knees.

ask: • **Why do you think Peter lost his trust in Jesus and started to sink?**
• **When did you lose courage or faith in something?**

say: **Before Peter could sink very far, Jesus reached out and grabbed Peter, and they both got into the boat.** Help kids re-enter the boats. When everyone is in a boat,

say: **Then the wind calmed down.** Have your helper turn off the CD and the fan.

say: **Listen to how quiet it is now.**
Lower your voice and

ASK: • **How did Peter show that he trusted Jesus?**
• **When was a time you trusted Jesus in a scary or hard situation?**
• **How can you show that you trust Jesus?**

say: **The Bible shows us the way to trust. Jesus taught Peter to trust him when Peter started to sink. We can trust Jesus to help us whenever we start "sinking" in real life. When we step out and try hard things, Jesus will be right there beside us. Let's pray and thank God for being so faithful.**

Close with a prayer similar to this one. Pray: **Dear God, thank you for giving us your Bible to teach us how to trust you more. Help us to trust you in any special ways that we need to. In Jesus' name, amen.**

Teacher Tip

You might want to have extra helpers to guide kids on the sea. By building the sea against one wall, you'll only have one side and the ends of the sea to monitor.

Teacher Tip

You might be tempted to use spray bottles of water to get the kids wet to enhance the atmosphere. But water will make the plastic very slippery. The fans and the sound effects, along with the noise created by kids walking on the plastic, will create enough of a really "stormy" atmosphere!

Teacher Tip

The plastic makes a noisy sea, but you'll find that it's worth it. After all the kids climb into the boats, the hush that will fall over the room will be powerful!

Bible Adventure 10

Men bring their friend to Jesus for healing

Bible Basis: Luke 5:17-25

Supplies

- assistant to operate the CD
- Bible-time robe for you
- stool
- "roof debris" (dry leaves, sticks, broken pieces of lumber)
- CD player with "repeat" function
- *Skits & Drama* CD: "Street Sounds" (track 18)
- small bag of pretzels
- 3 tan or brown sheets
- tacks
- scissors

Preparation

Create a Bible-times "room" by tacking two sheets to the walls in a corner of your room.

Cut a jagged hole in the third sheet, and use it to create a "ceiling" for your room by stretching it across the corner of the room. Let the rough edges of the hole hang down (see illustration). Scatter dried sticks and pieces of lumber under the hole as if it's rubble. Place a supply of dried leaves and small sticks on top of the "roof" where kids can still see them. Place the stool in the corner, out of the way.

Place the CD player nearby, preferably behind other objects in your room so your assistant can operate it unseen.

Wear a simple robe so you'll look like a person from Bible times. Your assistant—who hopefully won't be visible to the children—needn't be in costume.

Before kids enter the room, have your assistant play "Street Sounds" (track 18) on the *Skits & Drama* CD, setting the CD on "repeat" so it plays the track over and over.

Bible Adventure

As you meet children outside the room,

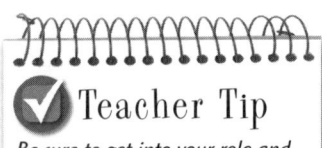

Teacher Tip

Be sure to get into your role and be slightly disappointed that the kids aren't the roofers you were expecting. You never specify who exactly you are, but be playful! Your attitude will help kids enter into the imaginary world you've created in your room.

say: **Hey, glad you're finally here. I thought you might need help finding the house. Um…where are your tools? Roofers need tools. You *are* the roofers come to repair the roof, right? No?**

Oh, then you must be reporters who heard what happened. I've had a *herd* of reporters coming by. But you're not reporters, either, because you don't have those little notebooks reporters carry around.

That must mean you're just…curious. You heard what happened and want to see where it took place. Well, OK…come on—I'll show you. The house is right through this alley.

Lead kids into the room. Stand in the corner, where the hole is above you. On the floor at your feet is rubble of broken boards, sticks, leaves…stuff you can easily kick out of the way.

say: **Sorry for all the rubble…I'll just clear some of this away.**

Well, here's where it happened. They did a number on that roof, I'll tell you that—knocked a hole right in it. It's terrible. First, listen…hear all that noise? You can hear every donkey passing by, every herd of sheep headed past. Motion to kids on one side of the room. **And if it rains, you'll know all about it over here. Plus, every time the breeze blows there's still stuff falling down. Better scoot back away from the hole until the roofers get here. I don't want anyone to get clobbered if a crossbeam comes down.**

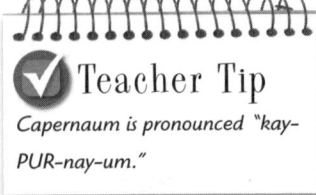

Teacher Tip

Capernaum is pronounced "kay-PUR-nay-um."

Are any of you from Capernaum? If so, you probably know that Jesus was here yesterday. *Right* here—in this room. Right here in this *corner*. This place was *packed* with people who'd come to hear Jesus teach and to see if he'd perform a miracle or two, maybe heal somebody.

It was so packed that…well, I'll show you. Everyone stand up. Now put your hands down at your sides and scoot toward the middle of the room until you're shoulder to shoulder with someone…now those of you in the front of the room stand firm and everybody else scoot up until your tummy is touching the back

64 Large-As-Life Bible Adventures

of the person in front of you. Pause. Now that's crowded! And that's how crowded it was in here yesterday!

The whole house was like that… and the yard, the whole *block*. Everyone wanted to see Jesus. Go ahead and "un-crowd" while I tell you the rest of the story. Pause.

Well, there were these guys who had a buddy. The buddy—I can't remember his name—was on a sort of stretcher, a mat. That's because the guy couldn't walk. I don't know what had happened to the guy, but he wasn't getting better. He was paralyzed—that means he couldn't move at all. The man needed friends to help him.

Here's what that's like…

Have kids form pairs. Give each child a small pretzel ⊕. **OK, now everyone hold on to your pretzel in one hand, and stretch out that arm. Pretend that arm is paralyzed. It can't move at all. So you can't bend your elbow, but you really want to eat the pretzel.**

Demonstrate how you have to keep your arm stiff and straight because you can't bend the elbow. You can't bring the pretzel to your mouth.

ASK: • **How are you going to eat the pretzel when your arm can't move?** Allow kids to try to figure it out. If they don't get it after one minute,

say: **Remember, you have your friends to help you!** If kids still don't get it, go over to a person and feed your pretzel to him or her. Then the idea will catch on. Partners must feed each other the pretzels. Their stiff arms will be able to reach a friend's mouth, and vice versa. After everyone has been fed a pretzel, tell kids they can move their arms normally now.

say: **Wow! We needed our friends so we could eat the pretzels. In our Bible story, the paralyzed man needed his friends to bring him to Jesus.** Take a seat on the stool.

Why sit on a stool? Two reasons: If you're at all tall, children sitting on the floor at your feet have to crane their necks to see you, and that position quickly becomes uncomfortable. Also, sitting with kids signals being comfortable and familiar, and it lets you lean toward children seated on the floor without having to actually jump up and down repeatedly during the session.

say: **With so many people trying to see Jesus, there was no way the friends carrying a stretcher could make it through the door. They couldn't even get *close*. But these guys were going to be sure their buddy saw Jesus—period.**

Men bring their friend to Jesus for healing

Here's what they did: They circled around the back of the house and found the stairs up to the roof. And when they got up there they started digging—right through the roof! They ripped up the tiles...then they dug down between the rafters...stuff came falling down...right here in front of Jesus! Point to the rubble.

When the hole was big enough, the friends lowered the mat right down to where Jesus was standing. Boy, those are some friends! They were even willing to get in trouble to make sure their buddy met Jesus.

ASK: • **What's a great thing some friend has done for you?**

say: **Maybe your friend got a new video game, and he loaned it to you even though he hadn't played it yet. Or maybe you have a friend whose family went on vacation, and she could take a friend with her to Disneyland—and she chose you!**

Allow each person a chance to answer. If you have a large class, have kids form pairs to answer the question, then invite volunteers to share their answers with the rest of the class.

say: **Sounds like you have some great friends! When the men lowered their friend to Jesus** (indicate a place on the floor just in front of you as you stand in the corner), **Jesus saw how much faith the friends had. He knelt down** (do this as you tell the story) **and said to the paralyzed man, "Friend, your sins are forgiven."**

That made the teachers of the law—they were in the audience right toward the front in the good seats—sit up and take notice. They stroked their beards—stroke your beards like this—and they said, "Hey, wait a minute. Only God can forgive sins. If Jesus is forgiving sins, then that means he thinks...he's God's Son or something!"

Jesus knew what they were thinking. Jesus said, "Which do you think is easier for me, to forgive this man's sins or to heal him? Tell you what—I'll do both so you know I am who I say I am."

Jesus looked at the paralyzed man and said, "Get up, take up your mat, and go home."

The paralyzed man lay there and he could...he could wiggle his toes! Have kids wiggle their toes with you. **He could wiggle his fingers!** Have kids wiggle their fingers. **He sat up...his legs were working, and his arms were working...and he stood up. His body worked perfectly!**

The friends on the roof? Well, I couldn't actually *see* them, but I'll bet they were going nuts! They were cheering and giving each other high fives...it's a wonder they didn't fall through the hole in the roof!

Do this: Give a high five to everyone around you! Yeah! Jesus healed this guy! Pause as kids give high fives.

Now, the guy with the mat didn't just go home—he went home jumping around and praising God and showing everyone how his feet worked. He was one happy, ex-paralyzed guy.

Jesus was his friend BIG time! Jesus forgave him his sins and made him walk!

ASK: • **In what ways is Jesus a friend to you?**

• **How can you be a friend to Jesus?**

Allow several minutes for kids to answer.

Then close in a group prayer, thanking God for sending Jesus to be our friend.

Men bring their friend to Jesus for healing

Bible Adventure 11

Jesus washes the disciples' feet

Bible Basis: John 13:1-17

Supplies

- Bible
- several bowls of warm water
- paper towels
- small plastic pool filled with sand
- large plastic trash bags
- a sign that reads "Upper Room"
- CD player
- small loaf of bread and a cup of grape juice (for props)
- *Skits & Drama* CD: "Servant Music" (track 19)
- several volunteers

Preparation

Before this lesson, enlist a volunteer to place a sign that reads "Upper Room" on the door of your meeting area as you're taking the kids on a brief search away from your room. Place a plastic pool filled with sand near the door. You may want to put large plastic trash bags underneath the pool to make cleanup easier. Set the bread and grape juice to one side. Prepare the bowls of warm water, and set them and the paper towels aside.

Bible Adventure

Meet kids as they gather outside the closed door to your room. Have kids remove their shoes and socks. Open your Bible to John 13:1-17, and show kids the passage.

say: **In today's Bible story, Jesus asked his disciples to find a certain room where they would share a special meal. Let's go on our own adventure right now to find that room.**

Lead the kids on a brief (and barefooted!) follow-the-leader search. While leading the kids,

ASK: • **Why do you think Jesus wanted to find a special room?**

Lead kids back to the outside of your room, and point out the sign indicating the "Upper Room."

say: **Here it is! You know, in Bible times the roads were made of dirt, so when people walked, their feet got very dirty. Each of you can step into the dirt in this pool before entering the Upper Room.**

Have kids step in the sand and then go into the room and sit down.

say: **Jesus knew that he didn't have much time left with his friends. He knew that the time was coming when he would die. So he gathered his closest friends in the Upper Room to have a special meal.**

ask: • **When guests come to your house, how do you welcome them?**

say: **In Bible times, people's feet got really dirty from walking on dirty streets all day. So when you were a guest at someone's house, the hosts would have a servant wash your dusty, dirty feet.**

ask: • **What do think it would be like to wash someone's dirty feet?**

Point to the bread and juice; then

say: **Jesus and his friends ate together. Then Jesus got up and did something amazing. Without saying anything, Jesus—God's Son—washed his disciples' feet! Let's see what the disciples might have felt like.**

With your volunteers, begin to wash kids' feet.

ask: • **What's it like to have someone wash your feet?**
• **Did anyone not want to have his or her feet washed? Why?**

say: **When Jesus got to Peter, Peter said, "No, you will never, ever wash my feet."**

ask: • **Why do you think Peter would refuse to let Jesus wash his feet?**

say: **Jesus told Peter that he must wash Peter's feet if Peter wanted to be a follower of Jesus.**

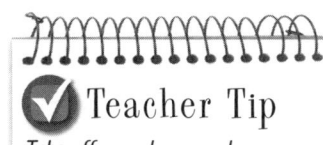

Teacher Tip

Take off your shoes, and encourage any helpers to do the same. The more you participate in the learning experience, the more meaningful it is for the kids (and the more fun for you!).

Jesus washes the disciples' feet

Finish washing the kids' feet.

say: **There's some people in the room who haven't had their feet washed.** Pause for kids to discover that you're referring to yourself and your volunteers.

ask: • **What should we do?**

Let kids wash your own and your volunteers' feet; then

ASK: • **What was it like washing a leader's feet?**
• **Why do you think Jesus would wash his disciples' feet when that's a job only servants did?**

say: **Jesus asked the disciples this same question. He said, "Do you understand what I was doing?" Then Jesus answered that question by explaining that he wanted to set an example for the disciples to follow.**

ask: • **What did Jesus want his disciples to do?**

say: **Jesus wanted his disciples to love others by serving them. Jesus wants us to love and serve others, too.**

Have kids form pairs or trios. Play the "Servant Music" (track 19) from the *Skits & Drama* CD. Ask the following questions, and have kids share responses within their pairs or trios.

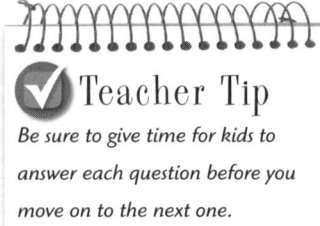

Teacher Tip
Be sure to give time for kids to answer each question before you move on to the next one.

ASK: • **What are some ways you can serve others?**
• **What are some ways you can love others?**
• **How is serving someone like loving that person?**

say: **Jesus gave us the best example of love and service. We can begin to practice that right now!**

After he washed the disciples' feet, Jesus said that his disciples would be blessed to serve others. Let's show our love for each other by helping others put on their shoes. First, find a partner, and see who's wearing the most blue. That person will be the helper first. Then you'll switch roles, and the other person will be the helper.

Have kids work in their pairs, helping put on each other's shoes. Be ready to assist any kids who might need help. After kids' shoes are back on, close in a prayer similar to this one. Pray: **Dear Jesus, thank you for giving such a wonderful example of love and service. We want to love and serve others, just as you did. Please show us special ways to love others, just as you do. In your name, amen.**

Large-As-Life Bible Adventures

Bible Adventure 12

Jesus dies on the cross and rises again

Bible Basis: Luke 23–24

Supplies

- Bible
- plastic sword
- dramatic volunteer to play the part of the Roman Guard
- simple Bible-times "guard" costume (such as a robe, sash, and sandals)
- photocopy of the "Guard's Script" (page 74)
- *Skits & Drama* CD: "He Is Risen" (Luke 24:5b-6a) (track 20)
- CD player

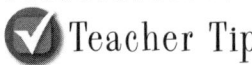

Teacher Tip

Kids may respond to the guard with a wide range of words, actions, and emotions. It's crucial that your guard is mature enough to aptly handle these responses and use them to guide children toward a powerful understanding of today's Bible story. Be sure to prayerfully select your volunteer for today's adventure.

Preparation

Contact a man or teenage boy in your congregation to be a Roman guard who interrupts your "secret meeting" of Christians and interrogates the students.

Give your volunteer a copy of the "Guard's Script" (page 74), and cue the guard so he'll know exactly when to interrupt you. The guard needs to be stern, but not so stern that younger students become too frightened. Give the soldier the sword and costume.

Choose a dark, sheltered place for your secret meeting room. It might be a dark stairwell or landing, a safe furnace room, or a corner of a balcony. The space should be a little cramped.

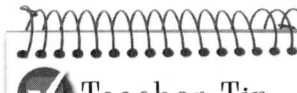

Teacher Tip

It will add great surprise and mystery to recruit a "soldier" who is unfamiliar to your kids. This is not the time to use your pastor or anyone easily identified by your children. Whomever you choose, be sure he is prepared to play off of the kids' answers—those are not scripted!

Bible Adventure

When kids arrive, gather them in a tight huddle by the door. Appear agitated and keep glancing up and down the hall as you say in hushed tones: **It's no longer safe for us to meet in this room. Today we're transporting back to Bible times, and there are Roman guards everywhere looking for followers of Jesus. I've found a secret room where I think we'll be safe. Stay close and follow me!**

Take about two minutes to lead kids in a circuitous route around the church building to arrive at your secret room. Be sure to take your Bible with you.

Build in lots of suspense. If you encounter someone in the halls, have kids back up against a wall and freeze. Stop at every corner and peek around before you signal the kids to follow you.

When you arrive at your secret room, have everyone take several deep breaths. Have kids huddle around you as you say in an anxious voice: **I think we'll be safe here. But we'll have to speak softly. A few minutes before you showed up I ran into Peter, one of Jesus' disciples. He looked scared, and he said there are Roman soldiers and Temple guards *everywhere*!**

Maybe you don't know what's happened lately, so I'll tell you. Jesus was arrested! Some of the Jewish leaders didn't like Jesus calling himself God's Son, so they had the Romans grab Jesus. The Roman soldiers took Jesus to a hill outside Jerusalem and hung him on a cross to die.

Since Jesus was killed, all of Jesus' disciples have been in hiding. They're afraid that Roman soldiers might come and arrest them. We need to be in hiding, too, even though we love God. That's why we're meeting in this secret place…

Have the Roman Guard interrupt you at this point. If the children answer the guard's questions, that's great. If no one speaks up, feel free to answer the questions yourself.

As the Roman Guard leaves, hold up your Bible and

say: **Jesus *did* rise from the dead. Jesus is more powerful than sin and death! We can read all about it in the Bible. I'm so glad that God loves us and sent his Son, Jesus! You know, we all disobey God and don't do the things God wants us to do. That's called sin. If we believe in Jesus, our sins can be forgiven by God. And we can live forever in heaven!**

We don't need to be afraid of Roman guards or of anything else anymore! I believe in Jesus—do you? And I love God!

Have kids form pairs or trios to discuss the following questions. After each question, invite volunteers to share their answers with the rest of the group. Play "He Is Risen"

Teacher Tip

Kids absolutely love the idea of sneaking to a secret room and being on the lookout for guards! It's a great way to capture the emotions of those involved in the real Bible adventure!

Teacher Tip

Hide your Roman Guard where you're sure he can see your group sneak by. That way, he'll be sure to know where to find you!

(Luke 24:5b-6a) (track 20) from the *Skits & Drama* CD softly in the background.

ask: • **How does it feel to know that Jesus rose from the dead? Why?**
• **Why do you think Jesus was willing to die on the cross for your sins?**
• **How can you thank Jesus for his love given to you?**

say: **Jesus died for you because he loves you. He rose from the dead to offer forgiveness for your sins, and to give you the chance to live with him forever in heaven. All you have to do is believe in him.**

Close in prayer, thanking God for the incredible gift of Jesus, and asking him to help each child in your class grow closer to Jesus.

Teacher Tip

When the Roman Guard gruffly asks if your children know Jesus, you might be surprised to find that many children (even those from "churched" families) answer with a wide-eyed "No!" This is a great teachable moment! Ask the guard to interrogate one of the adults for a moment, while you huddle with the kids and say, "Jesus stood up for us when he went to the cross to die for our sins. Now we have the chance to stand up for him. Is pretending we don't know God's Son any way to show we love him?" Let children reconsider, and then call the Roman Guard back over.

Teacher Tip

If your secret room is really cramped, you may want to move into an adjacent room or hallway after the Roman Guard leaves.

Guard's Script

Practice the lines and actions below. Meet with the leader ahead of time to find out where kids will be meeting. Hide somewhere near the meeting place but out of kids' view so you can hear them.

When the leader says, "That's why we're meeting in this secret place…" burst into the room and deliver your lines. Pause to let children answer the bulleted questions.

(Pound on the door or wall of the secret meeting room, then burst in.)

I thought I heard some commotion in here. Halt in the name of Caesar!

- **What are you doing here?**

- **Are you followers of this Jesus who's been crucified?**

- **All of Jerusalem is in an uproar about this man, Jesus. Who exactly was he? What did he do that's so special?**

- **When was the last time you were with Jesus?**

- **What can you tell me about a man named Peter?**

You may know that Jesus was crucified last Friday for offenses against the Jewish God. This morning it was discovered that his body is missing. Several of his followers claim that he has risen from the dead. Whenever we crucify anyone *(slap the sword against a wall)*, **we make sure they're good and dead.**

(continued on next page)

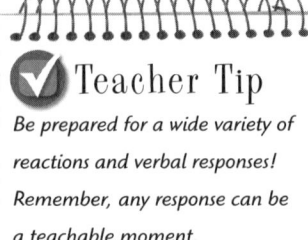

Teacher Tip
Be prepared for a wide variety of reactions and verbal responses! Remember, any response can be a teachable moment.

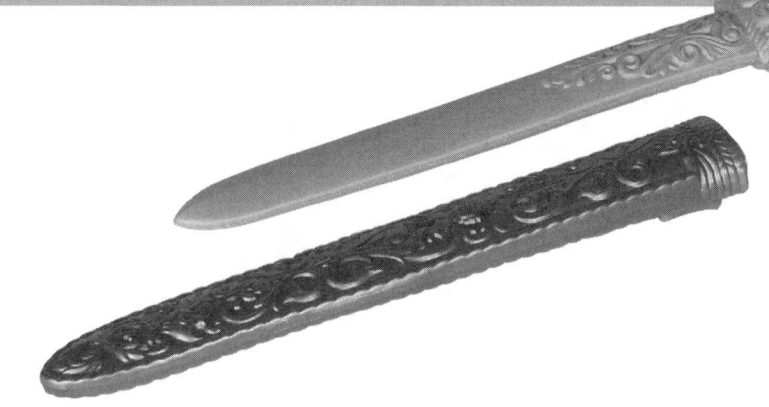

(continued from previous page)

(Change your tone from intimidating to thoughtful.)

- **How do you think such a thing could happen?**

One of the soldiers guarding Jesus' tomb is a friend of mine. He told me that he saw an angel appear, felt an earthquake, and then passed out from fear. When he woke up, the huge stone in front of the tomb was rolled away, and Jesus' body was gone!

- **What do you people think of all this?**

- **I don't know what I believe anymore. What do you people believe? Who is this Jesus?**

Hmm. Maybe Jesus really *is* the Son of God. Well, my commander isn't happy about Jesus' body disappearing. If I were you, I'd stay out of sight for a few more days. I'm going to let you go—but don't let me catch you again.

(Exit from the room.)

Permission to photocopy this handout from *Large-As-Life Bible Adventures* granted for local church use. Copyright © Group Publishing, Inc., P.O. Box 481, Loveland, CO 80539.

Bible Adventure **13**

Jesus appears to his followers as they fish

Bible Basis: Matthew 28:18-20; John 21:1-17

Supplies

- Bible
- masking tape
- 25-foot length of light nylon rope
- 25-foot lengths of clothesline (1 length for each group of five kids)
- flashlight for each group of five kids
- yellow, red, or orange tissue paper to tape over the illuminated end of the flashlights (to create a "mini-campfire" for each group)
- fish-shaped crackers
- paper cups
- *Skits & Drama* CD: "Fish Fry" (track 21) and "Breakfast by the Sea" (track 22)
- CD player

Preparation

Before kids arrive, create a "Sea of Galilee" like the one in the diagram. It should comfortably seat all the children who'll come to class. Also make sure all the flashlights are working properly. Tape yellow, red, or orange tissue paper over the illuminated end of the flashlights. Put fish-shaped crackers in paper cups so each group of five kids will have some to share.

Bible Adventure

As kids gather by the door to your room, greet them warmly.

When you're ready to begin,

say: **Thanks for coming today! I'm glad you're here. In fact, I'm so glad you're here that I'm going to give you the ultimate honor: I'm declaring you all honorary fish! Let's see your best "fishy faces."**

Encourage children to impersonate fish.

say: **OK, fish, keep those fish faces going while you swim as fish into the room and sit in groups of about five.**

Lead kids into the room making swimming motions, and help kids sit in groups of five inside the masking-tape "Sea of Galilee."

Teacher Tip
If you have a small class, let kids form trios.

say: **Let me give you some background before we get into today's Bible story. Before today's story took place, Jesus had died. Some tough-looking Roman guards were looking for any of Jesus' followers—particularly a man named Peter. Peter was a fisherman and a close follower and friend of Jesus.**

When Jesus was arrested, Peter ran away and hid. He was afraid of those Roman soldiers! And Peter was sad—he was sure he'd never see Jesus again. But then Jesus rose from the dead! Peter was overjoyed when Jesus appeared alive again!

But Peter wasn't sure what to do next. So Peter—who was a fisherman before Jesus asked him to be a disciple—did what he'd always done. He went fishing! And he took some of the other disciples with him.

Open your Bible to John 21 and show it to the kids.

say: **Before Jesus went back to heaven, he appeared to his disciples many times. Today we'll learn about one time that was very special to Peter. To do that I need one group to be in an instant Bible drama.** Select one of the groups that has at least four people in it. If you have small class, you may have to combine two groups.

Cast one person to be Jesus. Ask three of the group members to be Peter, Thomas, and Nathanael. If there are more group members, let them be "fish" along with all the other children.

Place "Jesus" at one side of your "stage" area. Stand "Peter," "Thomas," and "Nathanael" up front and center, facing the audience, as if they're standing in a boat. Point out to them that they can't cross the masking tape line. Give Peter a 25-foot length of nylon rope.

Teacher Tip
It's important to have a boundary that the "fish" can't leave. Remember, fish need to stay in the water! Be sure to create a back boundary to your "lake" that's no more than 10 feet from where the disciples stand... or they'll never catch the fish!

Also, demonstrate to the disciples how to toss the rope. You'll loosely loop it in your right hand, holding one end of the rope in that hand. You'll hold the other end of the rope with your left hand. Toss the rope by sweeping your right hand from left to right, releasing the loops. The rope will fly up and across the fish, snaring some of them.

Teacher Tip

You might be tempted to use a real fishnet. Don't do it. Children will feel trapped when it closes over them and will fight against it. They will quickly become ensnared, and you'll lose control of the group. Use a "fishing line" rope instead.

say: **All of you in the audience have a part, too: You're the fish! Let's see you make your best fishy faces again.** Pause. **Good job! Now, fish don't talk, so you'll have to act out your part without speaking. Fish need water, so you've got to stay in the lake. See that shoreline?** Point to your boundaries. **And fish don't walk, so you'll have to move by "scootching" on your bottoms. Scootch into the left side of the lake, and stick close together. You're a school of fish, so you stick close and stay together.**

Peter, you and your friends have a "net" there. I'll show you how to use it. Demonstrate how to toss the rope and catch fish.

You disciples, don't toss the net until the narrator tells you to do so. And fish, listen so you know when to *silently* scootch around, and where. Ready? Let's listen and act along with the story as it unfolds.

Play the *Skits & Drama* CD: "Fish Fry" (track 21). When the track ends, lead everyone in a round of applause for a job well done. Ask groups to circle up again, and place the ropes where they won't be a distraction.

say: **After they finished eating breakfast, Jesus told Peter that Peter had a new job. Instead of fishing, Jesus wanted Peter to get busy sharing God's love. You see, fishing is a fine job, but Jesus wanted Peter to fish for *people*, not fish. It was time for Peter to get out of the boat and onto the shore where he could share God's love with people around him.**

Now we'll get a chance to share God's love with other people by playing a game called Stringer.

Show children and leaders a 25-foot length of clothesline. Demonstrate how to do the following activity as you describe it.

say: **It's easy. Each group will circle up and stay seated. Starting with the person wearing the most blue, you'll snake a length of clothesline though your clothes. It can go through your sandals, a belt loop, or even through a sleeve! Then you'll pass the clothesline on to the next person, who will do the same thing. Eventually the clothesline will connect everyone in your group, like the way God's love connects us.**

Here are three rules to keep in mind:

1. The rope must travel through at least one piece of clothing.

2. You can ask for and get help from a friend if you need it.

3. When you pass the rope to the person next to you, you must say at least one thing you appreciate about that person. For instance, I might say to [child's name], **"Your smile always makes me feel welcome. Thanks for sharing God's love with**

me by welcoming me every day."

Ready? Circle up and let's give it a try. You'll have about five minutes to get around the circle.

Give each group a length of rope.

Provide two- and one-minute countdowns so children will know to wrap up the activity. Once groups have finished, encourage them to share a "group hug" and then carefully and *slowly* (beware of rope burn!) remove the clothesline and return it to you.

say: **You did a great job! Let's celebrate by having our own "breakfast on the beach" as you talk in your groups.**

Ask one person from each group to come and get paper cups with fish-shaped crackers  in them to carry back and share with their groups. Also give each group a flashlight to serve as a "campfire."

Dim the lights in the room, and play *Skits & Drama* CD: "Breakfast by the Sea" (track 22) as groups discuss the following questions. Invite volunteers to share their answers with the rest of the class.

ASK: • **We decided to share our snack. But what if I'd kept it all to myself? How would you have felt? How is that like not sharing God's love?**

• **Why do you think God wants to share his love with us?**

• **How has someone shared God's love with you?**

• **How can you share God's love with someone this week?**

After a few minutes, encourage kids to wrap up their conversations. Close in prayer, thanking God for sharing his love with us by sending Jesus.

Teacher Tip

Some children are more sensitive about their bodies and drawing attention to themselves than others. Monitor the activity and be sure that children who are self-conscious can participate at a level in which they're comfortable. Snaking the rope through a shoe or watchband counts!